Cooking with Kids™

Just 5 Ingredients

Healthy Recipes for Busy Families on the Go!

Kelly Lambrakis

Copyright 2015   Twenty-Three Publishing

www.CookingWithKids4YourHealth.com

Black and White Interior Version

ISBN-13: 978-0-9968131-4-3

Cover Design by Laurel Lane

Preface

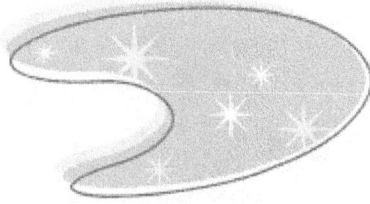

As a working mom with three very active boys, I understand the concern of trying to get meals on the table during busy hectic schedules.   Our family makes it a priority to stay away from processed foods, and eating fresh foods as much as possible.   So the challenge always seems difficult when healthy eating is a priority and there is little time to spend in the kitchen.

Over a year ago, I started on a unique culinary-journey, revisiting all of my favorite family recipes.   My goal was to make them healthier and easier to prepare, using only whole foods, without any processed or packaged ingredients. In addition, I wanted them to be simple enough to make, even when time was limited.   The outcome became a special compilation of delicious and healthy recipes that my whole family loves to make and eat. So with much anticipation, *Cooking with Kids - Just 5 Ingredients* was created.

I'm very excited to share this cookbook with you. My hope is for adults and children everywhere to explore the many options of healthy eating, realizing that it doesn't take much time or effort to cook wholesome and delicious meals that the whole family will love.

~ Kelly Lambrakis

In the Kitchen

Introduction

Cooking with Kids - Just 5 Ingredients, is the result from my own personal experience, in addition to the many requests from those who have our first two cookbooks.

We found that although many families love cooking together, sometimes there just isn't enough time to a make a healthy meal that everyone will appreciate. We set out to make a healthy cookbook for everyone to enjoy, even for the busiest of families on the go. As a result, ***Cooking with Kids - Just 5 Ingredients*** was proudly created.

This cookbook will not only introduce adults and children to the kitchen, but also teach healthy eating habits that will last a lifetime. Each healthy whole food recipe has no more than 5 ingredients (excluding water, non-stick cooking spray, salt, pepper and spices).

Cooking with Kids - Just 5 Ingredients will give a beginner's understanding of healthy cooking and baking, allowing you to follow and understand recipes with simple, step-by-step instructions.

All of these recipes have been made and selected by the pickiest of eaters. You will find them easy to prepare and high in nutrition. In addition, they are very fun to make and eat too! Although, some children may be able to make these recipes on their own, most kids will need additional hep from an adult, depending on their age and cooking level.

This cookbook also has interesting food facts, including unique 2D barcodes, like the image above, that can be scanned with a smart phone to access fun and interactive information and entertainment related to cooking. You can download a free QR reader app directly from your phone's app store. As always, kids should ask their parents for permission.

Enjoy!

Health Benefits of
Organic Cooking

Children need nutritious food to help them grow. As a family, we try to eat healthy and organic foods whenever possible. Our children's growing brains and bodies are far more susceptible to toxins than adults, so we believe there is no better reason to cook organic other than for the main fact that it is so much healthier for you. Organic foods are free of man-made chemicals, poisons, and pesticides. Also organic meat, poultry, eggs, and dairy products come from animals that are not given antibiotics or growth hormones.

Many people claim that organic food tastes better, and that they feel a noticeable boost in their overall health and energy level when the majority of the food they consume is organic. Great nutrition means maximizing on the freshest and most pure ingredients, drinking clean water, and listening to the feedback that your body gives you. It means eliminating or minimizing preservatives, synthetic chemicals, refined sugars, refined empty carbohydrates, saturated fats and acidic foods.

Cooking with Kids and their cookbooks support eating organic foods whenever possible. Although we are aware that it is more expensive to buy organic, we have found that as a family, we actually spend less overall on food, since we have chosen to cook more at home instead of eating out as often. Therefore, we encourage you to use your best judgment when deciding what works best for you and your family's needs.

Each recipe in this cookbook contains an approximate nutritional analysis. Optional ingredients are not calculated in the analysis. If a choice of ingredient is offered, the first ingredient is always used.

Early lessons in nutrition can develop healthy eating habits that last a lifetime. We have found that most kids acquire a natural preference for what they eat most often. The challenge is to make these healthy choices fun and appealing. We hope that the recipes in this cookbook provide just that, and help you and your family to a lifetime of healthy eating.

Cooking with Healthy Sugar Substitutes

If you would like to limit refined sugars and avoid artificial sweeteners, we encourage you to experiment with the numerous natural organic alternative sweeteners that are available in the market these days. Substitutes like fructose and sucrose still contain high levels of sweetness, that can affect the body in ways that normal sugar does, but there are definitely some natural sugar substitutes that are actually good for you and healthier than table sugar. Here are a few natural sugars that we enjoy cooking with. We recommend experimenting with any of these in our recipes that calls for refined sugar. You may be pleasantly surprised!

Coconut Sugar is a whole food that comes directly from the coconut. It is one of the healthiest sweeteners available. Coconut sugar produces delicious muffins, cookies, cakes, and healthy desserts. There is no taste of coconut from the sugar and it's the closest taste available of all the natural sweeteners to white, refined sugar. It can be substituted one for one with regular sugar. It is light brown in color and is not as fine as white sugar. However, it dissolves completely into your baked treats just like white refined sugar does.
Health Benefits: It is a great sweetener to use when making high energy snacks for kids so they will maintain their energy and mood throughout the day. Coconut sugar is not processed or refined, free from additives and chemicals. This sweetener has many vital minerals in it such as nitrogen, phosphorus, potassium, chlorine, magnesium and micro nutrients. It is particularly high in potassium, zinc and iron. It also contains rich B complex vitamins. *Coconut sugar has a very low glycemic index of 35, compared to sugar (sucrose) of 65.*

Fruit Puree is a healthy substitute that can be included in a number of baked goods. Choose fruits that are soft and offer a mild flavor such as dates, figs and bananas. For best results when replacing sugar in baked goods, combine these fruits with a small amount of water to create a puree before incorporating them in your recipe.
Health Benefits: A cup of date puree in place of a cup of sugar increases fiber content. It also lowers the calories in baked goods by as much as 500 calories.

Honey is almost 50% sweeter than sugar. When used in baking, replace ½ cup of honey for every 1 cup of sugar in your recipes. The final product will brown sooner than it does with sugar. You will have to regulate the temperature at least 25° lower and watch it closely to prevent it from burning. When used in cakes and other such recipes, the final product is definitely moister than it would be with the use of white sugar.
Health Benefits: Honey contains antioxidant compounds, is high in potassium and may help reduce sore throats. Raw honey is rich in B vitamins and also vitamin C. *Pure honey has a typical ranking of 58 on the glycemic index, compared to sugar (sucrose) of 65.*

Maple Syrup You would assume that maple syrup can be used only as an accompaniment to your waffles and pancakes. However, you can use pure maple syrup to sweeten your other baked goodies too. The darker the maple syrup, the stronger it is. Also, the darker maple syrup is better as a substitute for baking. If you are substituting maple syrup for white sugar, use 3/4 cup of real maple syrup for every cup of sugar the recipe calls for. Also decrease the total amount of liquid in the recipe by about 3 tablespoons for each cup of maple syrup you use. Baked goods will also brown much faster, so bake for less time or lower the temperature of the oven by 25°.

Health Benefits: 100% pure maple syrup is a whole food that is good for our bodies. It's great for your immune system, particularly with children. 2 ounces of maple syrup supplies up to 50% of our daily amount of manganese, iron and zinc and is high and omega-6 fatty acids. *Pure maple syrup has a medium glycemic index of 54, compared to sugar (sucrose) of 65.*

Here are two other alternative sweeteners that you also may want to try. They are both sugar alcohols. Although the word "alcohol" is part of their name, they cannot get you drunk. Many times these sweeteners are confused with being artificial, due to their chemical sounding names. While this is typically a good instinct when looking at ingredient labels, these two sugar substitutes are certainly not artificial. They are all natural and definitely ones to consider using in your favorite sweet recipes.

Erythritol is a natural sugar alcohol. It is found in some fruits and fermented foods. Erythritol is only about 70% as sweet as table sugar, so you'll need to account for that difference when baking.

Health Benefits: Erythritol has almost no calories and won't decay your teeth. Also, in moderate quantities, it doesn't cause the stomach upset that other sugar alcohols do. *All natural erythritol doesn't affect blood sugar, with a low glycemic index of zero, compared to sugar (sucrose) of 65.*

Xylitol is a natural sugar alcohol that can be found in fruits and vegetables. It looks and tastes much like sugar. It is produced from the bark of birch trees. Substitute xylitol one for one when used as an alternative to sugar in your favorite baked recipes. Although unlike erythritol, xylitol can sometimes have a laxative effect and shouldn't be consumed in excess.

Health Benefits: Xylitol has about 9 calories per teaspoon. It also prevents bacteria causing plaque to stick to teeth, which is why it's often used in sugar-free gum and can help prevent tooth decay. *All natural xylitol has a low glycemic index of 13, compared to sugar (sucrose) of 65.*

The glycemic index is a measurement of how quickly a certain food will raise your blood sugar. It is based on the amount of glucose in the food, because that is the carbohydrate most readily available and the fastest to have an impact on blood sugar levels. Eating too much high glycemic index foods can contribute to heart disease, diabetes and obesity. Foods are ranked as having a low glycemic index if they measure 55 or lower. Medium glycemic index foods range from 56 to 69, and high glycemic index foods are ranked at 70 or above.

Serving Sizes for School Age Kids

The following is a list of wholesome foods that young adults should be encouraged to eat daily. If one learns to enjoy them early, most likely they will be a healthy eater for life.

Whole Grain Bread, Cereal, Rice and Pasta Whole grain foods such as air-popped popcorn, bagels, bran cereals, brown rice, cornbread, whole grain bread, crackers, English muffins, low fat granola, macaroni, oatmeal, and spaghetti. The healthy eating pyramid recommends 1 piece or serving of a whole grain food at most meals. The use of white rice, white bread, potatoes, pasta and sweets should be limited.

Vegetables - Vegetables such as broccoli, carrots, cauliflower, celery, corn, fresh beans, green bell peppers, peas, potatoes, red bell peppers, spinach, squash, sweet potatoes, tomatoes, and zucchini. The healthy eating pyramid recommends at least 6 ounces or 3 servings of vegetables daily.

Fruits - Fruits such as apricots, berries, cherries, citrus fruits, dried fruits, kiwis, mangoes, melons, papayas, peaches, pears, pineapples, and plums. The healthy eating pyramid recommends 4 ounces or 2 to 4 servings daily.

Milk, Cheese and Yogurt - Dairy foods such as buttermilk, cottage cheese, cream cheese, plain and fruit flavored yogurt, ice milk, milk, ricotta cheese, Parmesan, string cheese and mozzarella. The healthy eating pyramid recommends 2 to 3 servings, with each serving being 8 ounces for non fat and low fat, and 4 ounces for whole fat.

Meat, Poultry, Fish, Dry Beans, Eggs, Nuts Protein such as chicken, extra lean ham, peanuts or reduced fat peanut butter, lean beef, lentils, split peas, beans: pinto, kidney, garbanzo, etc., shrimp, tofu, water-packed tuna, turkey, and walnuts. The healthy eating pyramid recommends 1 to 2 servings of poultry, fish and eggs with each serving being 4 ounces. Red meat is suggested to be used sparingly.

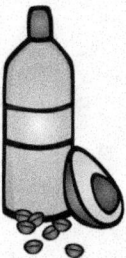

Healthy Oils - Plant oils such as olive, canola, soy, corn, sunflower, peanut, and other vegetable oils. The healthy eating pyramid recommends 2 ounces of plant oils daily.

Healthy Eating Pyramid

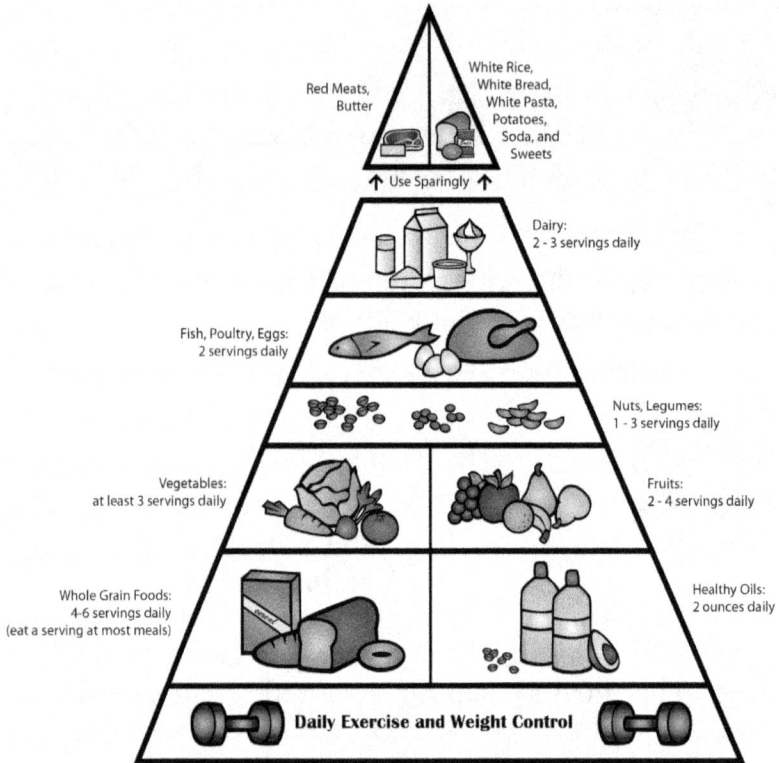

Red Meats, Butter

White Rice, White Bread, White Pasta, Potatoes, Soda, and Sweets

↑ Use Sparingly ↑

Dairy:
2 - 3 servings daily

Fish, Poultry, Eggs:
2 servings daily

Nuts, Legumes:
1 - 3 servings daily

Vegetables:
at least 3 servings daily

Fruits:
2 - 4 servings daily

Whole Grain Foods:
4-6 servings daily
(eat a serving at most meals)

Healthy Oils:
2 ounces daily

Daily Exercise and Weight Control

*Scan Me for more information
about the USDA healthy eating guidelines!*

Descriptions of Common Cooking Utensils and Baking Items

Baking Pan – A square or rectangular pan (glass or metal) used for baking and cooking food in the oven.

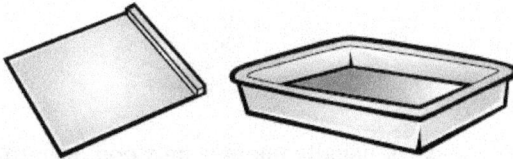

Baking Sheet – A flat metal sheet used for baking cookies or other items. Some have 1" sides, also called jellyroll pans.

Blender – An electric appliance used for blending liquids and grinding food.

Can Opener – A utensil used to open canned foods. Some are electric and some are used by hand.

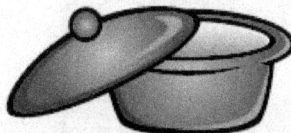

Casserole Dish – A glass or ceramic dish, usually 1 quart or 2 quart size, used to make casseroles or baked goods in the oven.

Colander – a metal or plastic bowl with holes, used to drain water or liquid from foods.

Cookie Cutter – a utensil used to cut dough or pie crust into desired shapes before baking.

Cutting Board – A board, usually made from wood or hard plastic, used for cutting or chopping ingredients on.

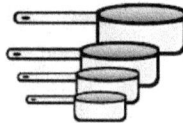

Dry Ingredients Measuring Cups - Cups of different measurements (1 cup, ½ cup 1/3 cup, and ¼ cup) used to measure dry ingredients like flour and sugar.

Electric Mixer - An electrical appliance used for mixing ingredients together.

Food Processor - An electrical appliance with a closed container and interchangeable blades that can chop, blend, shred, and puree foods at high speed.

Garlic Press - A tool used to crush cloves of garlic.

Grater - A utensil used to grate foods into fine strips or crumbs, like cheese.

Grill Pan - A skillet with ridges that is used to simulate grilling on the stove top

Ice Cream Scoop - A utensil used to remove ice cream from a carton or other container while forming the ice cream into a ball.

Juicer – manual or electrical device used for extracting the juice of fruits or vegetables.

Liquid Measuring Cup – A plastic or glass cup used to measure liquids, with various measurements printed on the side.

Measuring Spoons – Plastic or metal spoons in different sizes used to measure (tablespoon, teaspoon, ½ teaspoon, and ¼ teaspoon) either wet or dry ingredients.

Mixing Bowls – Bowls in various sizes in which you mix ingredients together.

Muffin Pan – Metal or glass pan with small or large round cups used for baking muffins and cupcakes.

Mixing Spoon – A medium or large spoon used for mixing and stirring ingredients.

Oven Mitt – Mittens or pads used to hold hot pots, pans, baking sheets, and plates. These are sometimes called hot pads or pot holders.

Paper Muffin Liner - An accordion-sided **paper** or foil cup in which muffins and cupcakes are baked and then removed for individual servings. These are also called cupcake cups or cupcake liners.

Pastry Brush – A small brush used to spread melted butter, margarine, egg yolk, or sauces over food.

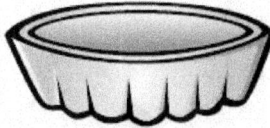

Pie Pan – A baking pan for pie, made of either glass or metal.

Pizza Cutter – A tool with a rolling cutter used to easily cut pizzas, dough, bread, or tortillas.

Potato Masher – A tool used to mash cooked potatoes, or anything soft to make them smooth.

Rolling Pin - A utensil consisting of a cylinder (usually of wood) with a handle at each end, used to roll out dough.

Saucepan – A pot with a handle used for stovetop cooking.

Serrated Knife – A sharp knife used for chopping and cutting firm foods.

Skillet or Frying Pan – A pan used on the stove for cooking food in hot fat or oil. Some skillets are non-stick and can be used for making pancakes.

Spatula – a flat, sometimes metal utensil used to lift and flip foods like pancakes, eggs, hamburgers and cookies. Some spatulas are rubber and used to fold foods together or scrape down batter from mixing bowls. Some rubber spatulas are also used for frosting cakes

Toaster – An appliance used for toasting bread.

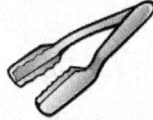

Tongs – A utensil used to grasp food so it can be moved, flipped, or rotated easily.

Vegetable Peeler - A special knife used to peel vegetables .

Vegetable Scrubber – A brush used to clean vegetables, like potatoes.

Whisk – A utensil used for mixing liquid ingredients, like eggs and milk.

Wooden Spoon – A spoon made out of wood used for mixing and stirring food.

Cooking and Baking Terms and Techniques

The following are important terms and techniques you may need to know before you start cooking or baking. If you are unsure of any cooking words, always ask an adult for help.

Aldente' – Food such as pasta or vegetables, cooked until tender but still firm, not soft.

Bake – To cook in an oven.

Beat – Mixing ingredients together with a fork, whisk, or mixer.

Boil – To heat liquid to the point that it bubbles vigorously.

Brown – Cooking food until it looks brown on the outside.

Chill – To place food in the refrigerator to make it cool.

Chop – To cut in small pieces on a cutting board.

Cooling Rack – A rectangular metal grid with small holes used to cool hot items on, like cookies.

Cream – To mix butter and sugar together until it becomes creamy.

Cube – To cut food in small square pieces.

Dash – A small amount of an ingredient such as salt and pepper, meaning to shake out in drops from a shaker.

Dice – Cut in cubes of the same small pieces.

Drain – To pour off the liquid through a colander or strainer.

Drizzle – To pour very small quantities of thin liquid over food.

Fold – To gently combine ingredients together from top to bottom until they are just mixed together, but not over mixed.

Grease – To spread the bottom and sides of a pan with cooking spray oil, shortening, butter or margarine. This keeps food from sticking to the pan.

Knead – To mix and work dough, usually with the hands, by folding, pressing, and squeezing.

Mince – To chop very finely.

Mix – To stir ingredients with a spoon.

Saute' – To fry briefly over medium to high heat.

Separating an Egg – Crack the egg on the edge of a bowl. Using your thumbs, gently open the shell in two halves. Pour the egg from one shell half to the other, letting the egg white fall into the bowl, while the yolk stays in the shell.

Simmer – To boil slowly at a low temperature.

Toss – Mixing ingredients by lifting them with a spoon or fork and then letting them drop back in the bowl. You do this when you mix green salad ingredients.

Whisk – To beat ingredients together with a wire whip until well blended.

*Scan Me for a fun cooking demo
of how to separate an egg!*

Equivalent Measures and Abbreviations

The information below shows measuring equivalents for teaspoons, tablespoons, cups, pints, fluid ounces, and more.

3 teaspoons = 1 tablespoon

4 tablespoons = 1/4 cup

5 tablespoons + 1 teaspoon = 1/3 cup

8 tablespoons = 1/2 cup

12 tablespoons = 3/4 cup

16 tablespoons = 1 cup (8 ounces)

2 cups = 1 pint (16 ounces)

4 cups (2 pints) = 1 quart (32 ounces)

8 cups (4 pints) = 1/2 gallon (64 ounces)

4 quarts = 1 gallon (128 ounces)

16 ounces = 1 pound

Dash or pinch = less than 1/8 teaspoon

Some of our recipes use abbreviations. Here are some common ones:

t = teaspoon

tsp. = teaspoon

T = tablespoon

Tbs. = tablespoon

c = cup

oz. = ounce

pt. = pint

qt. = quart

gal. = gallon

lb. = pound

= pound

Temperatures:

Fahrenheit	Celcius	Fahrenheit	Celcius
212°	100°	375°	190°
250°	120°	400°	200°
275°	140°	425°	220°
300°	150°	450°	230°
325°	160°	475°	240°
350°	180°	500°	260°

Safety in the Kitchen

1. Always have an adult nearby to help and supervise.

2. Always wash your hands before you start cooking. Also, wash your hands after handling raw meat.

3. Read the entire recipe before cooking to make sure you have all the necessary ingredients. Also check expiration dates on ingredients that can spoil.

4. Follow the recipes step by step. Missing a step may change your entire recipe.

5. If your recipe calls for fruits or vegetables, remember to always wash them thoroughly before beginning the recipe.

6. When cutting raw meat and poultry, use a cutting board that is used only for meat and poultry. Other utensils and cutting boards should not be touching raw meat and poultry. They should be separate from other foods because they may have germs that can make you sick.

7. Children should not cook anything on the stove, in the oven or microwave without adult help.

8. Always have an adult supervise when turning on appliances, like the stove, oven, blenders and mixers.

9. Always turn off mixers and unplug them when putting in or taking out beaters.

10. Keep all electrical appliances away from water to avoid shock. Never plug in appliances with wet hands.

11. Always ask an adult for help when using sharp knives or utensils.

12. Always turn pot handles on the stove away from yourself.

13. Always use oven mitts when handling hot things.

14. Ask an adult for assistance when taking hot pans in and out of the oven.

15. Always clean counter messes and spills immediately for safety and cleanliness.

Good Morning!

Crunchy Granola Wedges - 26

Breakfast Bites - 28

Florentine Skillet Hash - 30

Chocolate Chip Protein Pancakes - 32

Oatmeal Cottage Pancakes - 34

Bacon, Egg and Toast Cups - 36

Egg and Cheese Waffle Sandwich - 38

Oven Baked Cinnamon French Toast Sticks - 40

Turkey Sausage Breakfast Patties - 42

Apple Stuffed Strata - 44

*Scan Me for a cooking demo
of how to make a healthy
breakfast burrito!*

Crunchy Granola Wedges

Ingredients:

1 cup rolled oats	½ cup honey
1 cup cooked quinoa	1 cup dried cranberries
1 cup sunflower seeds	Pinch of salt
or any chopped nuts	Non-stick cooking spray

Equipment:

Large mixing bowl

Measuring spoons

Mixing spoon

Measuring cups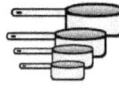

Rubber spatula

9" pie pan

Colander

Oven mitts

Directions:

1. Rinse quinoa thoroughly and cook according to package directions. Set aside to cool completely.

2. Preheat oven to 400°F.

3. In a large mixing bowl, gently mix the rolled oats, cooked quinoa, sunflower seed or nuts, honey, cranberries and salt together.

4. Prepare a 9" pie pan by spraying the bottom and sides with the cooking spray.

5. Immediately pour the mixture into prepared pie pan, and press down, using your fingers or a rubber spatula.

6. Bake for 10 to 15 minutes or until the granola is golden on top.

7. Using oven mitts, carefully remove the pie pan from the oven.

8. Cool for 30 minutes before cutting into wedges. These can be individually wrapped in plastic wrap and stored at room temperature for 3 days or frozen up to a month.

Makes 8 servings.

Nutrition per serving: *279 calories, 10 grams protein, 47 grams carbohydrates, 6 grams fat, 8 grams fiber*

Did you know? ...

Quinoa (pronounced keenwa) is a complete gluten free grain (although really a seed) and protein, which means that it contains all 8 essential amino acids. It is an excellent source of antioxidant vitamin E, which is needed for the body's healing process. It contains lots of immunity-enhancing minerals including zinc. It also contains lycine which helps fight off viral infections.

Breakfast Bites

Ingredients:

12 large eggs
1 ½ cups grated cheddar cheese
3 green onions, diced
½ cup red and green
   peppers, diced

Canadian bacon, diced (optional)
½ tsp. salt
½ tsp. pepper
Non-stick cooking spray

Equipment:

Medium
mixing
bowl

Liquid
measuring
cup

Mixing
spoon

Measuring
spoons

Serrated
knife

Cutting
board

Grater

Muffin
pan(s)

Whisk

Oven
mitts

Directions:

1. Preheat the oven to 350°F.

2. Grate cheese if needed. Set aside.

3. Prepare the muffin pan(s) by spraying the bottom and sides with cooking spray.

4. Using a serrated knife, carefully dice the onions, red and green peppers and Canadian bacon (optional), into small bite size pieces.

5. Spoon a few tablespoons of the vegetables, grated cheese and Canadian bacon into each of the 12 muffin cups, about two-thirds full.

6. In medium mixing bowl, carefully whisk together the eggs, salt and pepper.

7. Evenly distribute a spoonful at a time of the egg mixture over the vegetable and bacon pieces.

8. Bake for 15 to 20 minutes or until eggs are set and slightly golden on top.

9. Using oven mitts, carefully remove the pan from the oven. Cool before serving. These also may be frozen and reheated later.

Makes 6 servings (2 muffins per serving).

Nutrition per serving: 103 calories, 5 grams fat, 2 carbohydrates, 3 grams fiber, 15 grams protein

Did you know? ...

*An egg is one of the most nutritious food items in our diet.
It is rich in minerals, proteins and vitamins,
which is easily absorbed by the body.*

Florentine Skillet Hash

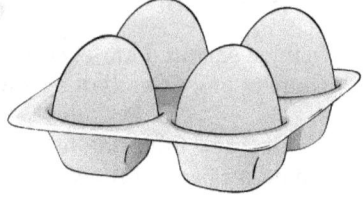

Ingredients:

2 cups frozen hash browns or
  pre-cooked shredded potatoes
2 cups fresh chopped spinach
4 large eggs

½ cup grated cheddar cheese
1 Tbs. olive oil
½ tsp. salt
½ tsp. pepper

Equipment:

Small
mixing
bowl

Measuring
cups

Measuring
spoons

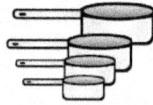

Whisk

Spatula

Non-stick
skillet or
frying pan
with a lid

Directions:

1. Grate the cheese if needed. Set aside.

2. In a medium size skillet, heat the olive oil on medium-low heat.

3. Evenly layer hash browns in the pan then layer the spinach on top.

4. In a medium mixing bowl, carefully whisk the eggs and pour on top of the spinach.

5. Sprinkle with the salt, pepper and grated cheese.

6. Cover the pan, reducing the heat to medium-low and cook until the potatoes are starting to brown on the bottom, the eggs are set and the cheese is melted, about 5 to 10 minutes.

7. Using a spatula, carefully cut into 4 wedges and serve immediately.

    Makes 4 servings.

Nutrition per serving: 226 calories, 12.4 grams fat, 12 carbohydrates, 3 grams fiber, 13.3 grams protein

Did you know? ...

A hash is a dish consisting of diced potatoes, eggs, spices and sometimes meat, that are mixed together and then cooked either alone or with other ingredients, such as onions. The name is derived from the French word "hatcher" which means "to chop".

Chocolate Chip Protein Pancakes

Ingredients:

4 large eggs
2 large ripe bananas
Non-stick cooking spray

¼ tsp. baking powder
¼ cup chocolate chips
Butter (optional)
Whipped Cream (optional)

Equipment:

Medium mixing bowl

Non-stick skillet or griddle

Whisk

Measuring cups

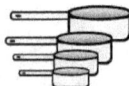

Fork

Measuring spoons

Spatula

Directions:

1. Peel the bananas and put them in the mixing bowl. Mash well with a fork so that there are little to no lumps.

2. Crack the eggs, and add them one at a time, whisking until everything is combined.

3. Add the baking powder and mix thoroughly.

4. Prepare the pan with non-stick cooking spray. Heat the griddle to medium high heat.

5. Pour about ¼ cup batter onto the hot pan. Sprinkle a few chocolate chips evenly onto each pancake. Cook for about 1 to 2 minutes or until golden brown.

6. Flip the pancakes over with a spatula. Cook for about 1 to 2 minutes more until done.

7. Repeat the steps until all the pancakes have been made.

8. Serve pancakes with butter, whipped cream or warm maple syrup.

Makes 2 serving.

Nutrition per serving: 310 calories, 9.8 grams fat, 38 carbohydrates, 12.6 grams protein

Did you know? ...

Eggs have a larger number of proteins when compared with chicken, beef or milk.

Oatmeal Cottage Pancakes

Ingredients:

¾ cup quick cooking rolled oats
¾ cup low fat cottage cheese

6 egg whites
1 tsp. vanilla extract
1 tsp. ground cinnamon
(optional)

Equipment:

2 medium
mixing bowls

Fork

Non-stick
skillet or
griddle

Measuring
spoons

Whisk

Spatula

Measuring
cups

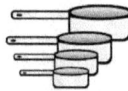

Directions:

1. Separate the egg whites from the egg yolks into two different medium size bowls. Refrigerate the yolks to use for another recipe.

2. Whisk the egg whites until frothy. Slowly stir in the rolled oats, cottage cheese, vanilla extract and cinnamon. Mix until everything is well combined.

3. Prepare the non-stick skillet or griddle with non-stick cooking spray. Heat to medium high heat.

4. Pour about ¼ cup batter onto the hot skillet or griddle. Cook for about 1 to 2 minutes or until golden brown.

5. Flip the pancakes over with the spatula. Cook for about 1 to 2 minutes more until done.

6. Repeat the steps until all pancakes have been made.

7. Serve with your favorite pancake topping.

Makes 2 serving.

Nutrition per serving: 325 calories, 3 grams fat, 43 carbohydrates, 11 grams fiber, 31 grams protein

Did you know? ...

Oats are a whole grain and high in soluable fiber, making them very healthy for children and adults.

Bacon, Egg and Toast Cups

Ingredients:

6 pieces whole grain
  sandwich bread
6 large eggs
½ cup low fat milk
½ cup grated swiss or
  cheddar cheese

½ cup pre-cooked and crumbled
  breakfast sausage or bacon
½ tsp. salt
½ tsp. pepper
Non-stick cooking spray

Equipment:

Medium
mixing
bowl

Whisk

Mixing
spoon

Measuring
spoons

Serrated
knife

Cutting
board

Grater

Muffin
pan - for
extra large
muffins

Liquid
measuring
cup

Oven
mitts

Directions:

1. Preheat the oven to 350°F.

2. Grate cheese if needed. Set aside.

3. Prepare the muffin pan by spraying the bottom and sides with cooking spray.

4. Using a serrated knife, carefully cut the crusts off the bread. Gently press each piece in the bottom and sides of the muffin pan cups.

5. Put a spoonful of crumbled bacon or sausage inside each bread cup.

6. In medium mixing bowl, carefully whisk together the eggs, milk, salt and pepper.

7. Evenly distribute a spoonful at a time of the egg mixture over the sausage or bacon. Sprinkle an equal amount of the cheese on top of the egg mixture.

8. Bake for 15 minutes or until eggs are set and cheese is melted.

9. Using oven mitts, carefully remove the pan from the oven. Cool before serving. These also may be frozen and reheated later.

Makes 6 servings.

Nutrition per serving: 184 calories, 6 grams fat, 24 carbohydrates, 2 grams fiber, 7.3 grams protein

Did you know? ...

*Breakfast is the most important meal of the day.
People who eat breakfast perform better at school and
have more energy during the day than people who skip breakfast.*

Egg and Cheese Waffle Sandwich

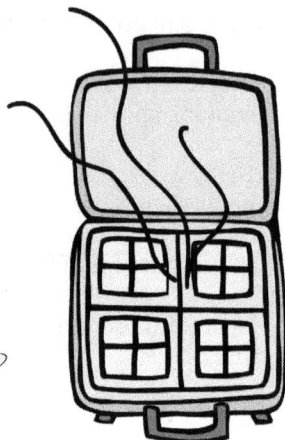

Ingredients:

4 toaster waffles
2 large eggs
2 slices jack or cheddar cheese

¼ tsp. salt
¼ tsp. pepper
Non-stick cooking spray

Equipment:

Small
mixing
bowl

Whisk

Baking
sheet

Measuring
spoons

Mixing
spoon

Oven
mitts

Directions:

1. Preheat the oven to 400°F.

2. Prepare the baking sheet by spraying with non-stick cooking spray.

3. Place the waffles on the baking sheet.

4. In a small mixing bowl, whisk the eggs with the salt and pepper, until well combined.

5. Carefully spoon egg mixture over waffles, spreading to fill cavities.

6. Bake for 10 to 12 minutes, or until eggs are set and waffles are crisp.

7. Using oven mitts, carefully remove the baking sheet from the oven.

8. Top two of the waffles with cheese. Cover with remaining two waffles and press together.

9. Let stand 1 minute to allow cheese to melt.

Makes 2 servings.

Nutrition per serving: 350 calories, 12 grams fat, 30 carbohydrates, 16 grams protein

Did you know? ...

The word "waffle" is from the Dutch, meaning "wafer."
In the late 1800's Thomas Jefferson returned from
France with the first waffle iron.

Oven Baked Cinnamon French Toast Sticks

Ingredients:

4 large eggs
½ cup vanilla low-fat
  Greek yogurt

1 tsp. ground cinnamon
4 wide-loaf slices bread
Non-stick cooking spray

Equipment:

Small and medium mixing bowls

Whisk

Mixing spoon

Cutting board

Serated knife

Measuring cups

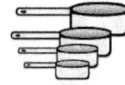

Baking sheet

Spatula

Oven mitts

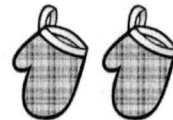

Directions:

1. Preheat the oven to 425°F.

2. Prepare the baking sheet by spraying with non-stick cooking spray.

3. Crack eggs into a medium mixing bowl. Whisk until blended. Carefully stir in yogurt and cinnamon until well combined.

4. Cut each slice of bread into 3 or 4 wide sticks. Quickly dip each bread stick into egg mixture. Place each piece on the baking sheet and lightly spray the tops with non-stick cooking spray.

5. Bake for 6 to 8 minutes or until crispy and golden brown on one side. Using oven mitts, remove the pan from the oven. With a spatula, carefully turn the bread pieces over.

6. Return to the oven for 6 to 8 more minutes, or until the other side is golden brown. Serve the French toast sticks with your favorite syrup or combine ingredients below to make this yummy dipping sauce:

Yogurt-Maple Dip

- ¾ cup vanilla low fat Greek yogurt
- ¼ cup natural maple syrup
- ½ tsp. ground cinnamon

Makes 4 servings.

Nutrition per serving: 173 calories, 7 grams fat, 18 carbohydrates, 2 grams fiber, 10 grams protein

Did you know? ...

French toast was created by medieval European cooks who needed to use every bit of food they could find to feed their families. They used day old bread and added eggs for additional moisture and protein.

Turkey Sausage Breakfast Patties

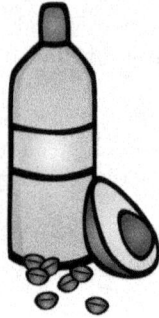

Ingredients:

2 Tbs. olive oil, divided
1 medium shallot, finely chopped
1 lb. lean ground dark meat turkey

1 ½ tsp. ground fennel seeds
1 ½ tsp. Kosher salt
1 tsp. ground black pepper
2 tsp. red pepper flakes (optional)

Equipment:

Medium mixing bowl

Measuring spoons

12" non-stick skillet

Mixing spoon

Serrated knife

Spatula

Cutting board

Directions:

1. Finely chop the shallot. Set aside.

2. Put 1 tablespoon of olive oil in the skillet and heat to medium-low.

3. Add the chopped shallots, stirring occasionally until soft, about 3 to 4 minutes. Let cool and set aside.

4. In a medium mixing bowl, combine the ground turkey, fennel, salt, pepper and red pepper flakes (optional). Add the cooled chopped shallots, mixing until just combined.

5. Using moist hands, form the mixture into 2-inch patties, making a total of 12 patties.

6. Put 1 tablespoon of olive oil in the skillet and heat to medium. Cook six patties at a time in the skillet until golden brown on each side, about 6 to 8 minutes.

7. Repeat with the remaining patties.

   Makes 6 servings.

Nutrition per serving: 105 calories, 2 grams fat, 4 carbohydrates, 18 grams protein

Did you know? ...

Fennel is a white or pale green bulb. It is crunchy like celery. The seeds taste like licorice or anise. Fennel is very high in folate, potassium and vitamin C, which is high in antioxidants and helps fight diseases.

Apple Stuffed Strata

Ingredients:

2 tsp. butter

4 cups Golden delicious apples cored and diced in ½" pieces

6 Tbs. sugar, divided

5 large eggs

2 tsp. cinnamon, divided (optional)

12 slices cinnamon swirl bread, cut into 1" cubes

1 ½ cups low fat milk

Non-stick cooking spray

1 cup chopped pecans or raisins, divided (optional)

Equipment:

Medium mixing bowl

Whisk

Large non-stick skillet

Measuring spoons

Mixing spoon

Liquid measuring cup

Serrated knife

11" x 7" glass baking pan

Cutting board

Oven mitts

Directions:

1. Carefully cut the bread into 1" cubes. Set aside. Core and dice the apples into ½" pieces. Set aside.

2. Melt butter in the skillet over medium-high heat. Add the diced apples and 1 tablespoon of sugar to the pan. Sauté for about 8 minutes or until the apples are tender and lightly browned. Remove from the heat and cool 5 minutes.

3. Spray the bottom and sides of the baking pan with the non-stick cooking spray. Arrange half of the bread cubes in the dish. Top with the apple mixture and top with ½ cup pecans or raisins (optional). Arrange the remaining bread cubes on top.

4. Combine the milk, eggs, 3 tablespoons sugar, and cinnamon in a medium bowl, stirring with a whisk until well blended.

5. Carefully pour the mixture over the bread. Cover the baking pan and chill for a few hours, or over night.

6. When ready to bake, preheat the oven to 350°F.

7. Uncover the dish, and sprinkle the remaining 2 tablespoons of sugar, 1 tablespoon of cinnamon and ½ cup pecans or raisins (optional) over the bread. Bake for 45 minutes to 1 hour, or until golden brown.

Makes 8 servings.

Nutrition per serving: 325 calories, 10 grams fat, 41 carbohydrates, 4 gram fiber, 12 grams protein

scan here for a cooking demo of how to peel, core and dice an apple!

Did you know? ...

A "strata" is an egg and bread layered dish, sometimes sweet and sometimes savory, made with cheeses, vegetables and meats, that is usually made for breakfast or brunch.

Soups, Salads, Sides and Sauces

Easy Baked Potato Soup - 46

Favorite Taco Soup - 48

Creamy Tomato Soup - 50

Crunchy Cucumber Salad - 52

Quinoa Kale Salad - 54

Crispy Corn Fritters - 56

Zucchini Parmesan Crisps - 58

Perfect Popovers - 60

Favorite BBQ Sauce - 62

Salsa di Pomodoro (Italian Tomato Sauce) - 64

Scan Me for a cooking demo of how to make a healthy chicken pasta salad!

Easy Baked Potato Soup

Ingredients:

8 large potatoes,
   peeled and cubed
3 Tbs. all purpose flour
3 Tbs. butter
6 cups milk
1 cup grated cheddar cheese

1 cup water or
   chicken broth (optional)
2 tsp. salt
2 tsp. pepper
Pre-cooked bacon, chopped (optional)
3 scallions, chopped (optional)

Equipment:

Large pot
or
saucepan

Mixing
spoon

Serrated
knife

Whisk

Cutting
board

Grater

Liquid
measuring
cup

Measuring
spoons

Directions:

1. Grate the cheese, if needed. Chop the scallions (optional). Carefully peel and cube the potatoes. Set aside.

2. In a pot on medium high heat, melt the butter. Gradually whisk in the flour until smooth. Stir in the milk a little at a time. Add the salt and pepper.

3. Turn the heat to medium low. Continue stirring until it starts to simmer, about 10 minutes.

4. Add the potatoes, then the water or chicken broth if desired. Continue to cook for 10 to 15 minutes more, or until potatoes are tender.

5. Slowly add the cheese, continuing to stir.

6. Serve the hot soup in bowls, garnished with chopped bacon and scallions, if desired.

Makes 12 servings.

Nutrition per serving: 220 calories, 12.3 grams fat, 12 carbohydrates, 1 gram fiber, 8 grams protein

Did you know? ...

Potatoes are grown more than any other food crop.
The average American eats over 125 pounds of potatoes a year!

Favorite Taco Soup

Ingredients:

1 lb. lean ground beef, chicken or turkey

2 cups frozen corn

2 cans (15 oz. each) black beans and/or red kidney beans, drained

2 cans (28 oz. each) tomato sauce

1 small onion, chopped

2 Tbs. packaged taco seasoning*

Tortilla chips (optional)

Grated cheese (optional)

or use our homemade recipe on page 96

Equipment:

Large pot or saucepan

Measuring cups

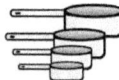

Mixing spoon

Measuring spoons

Can opener

Serrated knife

Colander

Cutting board

Directions:

1. Carefully chop the onion into bite size pieces.

2. In a large pot or saucepan, cook the ground beef, chicken or turkey on medium-high heat until the meat is browned, stirring to crumble.

3. Drain the meat mixture and return to the pot. Add the taco seasoning, mixing well to combine.

4. Carefully open the beans and tomato sauce with a can opener. Rinse and drain the beans well.

5. Add the beans, tomato sauce, chopped onions, and corn to the pot. Mix well with the meat mixture. Stir in a cup of water, depending on desired consistency.

6. Cook on medium-high heat for 15 to 20 minutes, or until heated through and soup starts to simmer, stirring occasionally.

7. Season with salt and pepper to taste.

8. Serve in bowls. Top with tortilla chips and grated cheese if desired.

Makes 8 servings.

Nutrition per serving: 195 calories, 4.3 grams fat, 22 carbohydrates, 7 grams fiber, 18 grams protein

Did you know? ...

Black beans are high in fiber and very good for you.
Their carbohydrates are used as a source of energy to fuel body functions such as your heartbeat, as well as physical activity.

Creamy Tomato Basil Soup

Ingredients:

4 cups chicken broth
1 can (28 oz.) tomato sauce*
6-8 fresh basil leaves, chopped
1 cup whole milk

1 tsp. salt
½ tsp. freshly ground black pepper
mini saltine or oyster crackers
(optional)

*or use our homemade
recipe on page 66*

Equipment:

Medium
or large
saucepan

Liquid
measuring
cup

Measuring
spoons

Mixing
spoon

Serrated
knife

Can
opener

Cutting
board

Directions:

1. Carefully chop the basil into bite size pieces. Set aside.

2. Open tomato sauce and chicken broth with a can opener, if needed.

3. Pour the tomato sauce and the chicken broth in a medium saucepan. Add the chopped basil, stirring until well combined.

4. Continue stirring over medium heat until soup starts to boil, about 5 minutes.

5. Reduce heat to low and slowly stir in milk.

6. Add the salt and pepper. Simmer gently for 15 minutes, stirring occasionally.

7. Serve hot in soup bowls, garnished with saltine or oyster crackers.

Nutrition per serving: 150 calories, 3 grams fat, 12 carbohydrates, 3 grams fiber, 4 grams protein

Did you know? ...

Tomatoes are often considered a vegetable, though in actuality they are a citrus fruit. Tomatoes contain important nutrients, such as niacin, folate and vitamin B6, that have associated with the reduction of heart disease risk.

Crunchy Cucumber Salad

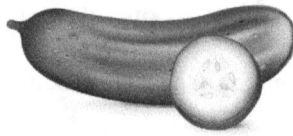

Ingredients:

15 Persian cucumbers, sliced
4 sprigs fresh dill, chopped
1 Tbs. honey

¼ cup apple cider vinegar
2 Tbs. extra virgin olive oil
1 Tbs. salt
½ tsp. freshly ground black pepper

Equipment:

Medium
mixing bowl

Whisk

Mixing
spoon

Measuring
spoons

Serrated
knife

Liquid
measuring
cup

Cutting
board

Directions:

1. Carefully cut the cucumbers into thin slices. Chop the dill. Set aside.

2. In a medium mixing bowl, slowly whisk oil with the vinegar. Add the honey, salt and pepper. Whisk until well combined.

3. Pour vinegar mixture over the sliced cucumbers and sprinkle with fresh dill.

4. Refrigerate for two to three hours before serving.

Makes 8 Servings.

Nutrition per serving: 70 calories, 2 grams fat, 7 carbohydrates, 2 grams fiber, 2 grams protein

Did you know? ...

Apple cider vinegar is excellent for your health. It creates an overall detoxification of your body. Research has also show that it can help stimulate cardiovascular circulation and help detoxify the liver. Cucumbers are an excellent source of vitamin K and a great source of the antioxidant vitamin C.

Quinoa Kale Salad

Ingredients:

1 cup quinoa
2 Tbs. extra virgin olive oil
2 Tbs. apple cider vinegar
1 bunch kale, chopped
½ cup sunflower seeds

½ cup dried cranberries
3 scallions, chopped (optional)
½ tsp. salt
½ tsp. freshly ground black pepper

Equipment:

Medium mixing bowl

Whisk

Mixing spoon

Liquid measuring cup

Cutting board

Measuring spoons

Serrated knife

Directions:

1. Cook quinoa according to package directions. Set aside to cool.

2. Chop the kale and scallions (optional) into bite size pieces. Set aside.

3. In a medium mixing bowl, whisk together the olive oil, vinegar, salt and pepper.

4. Add the cooled quinoa and chopped vegetables, sunflower seeds and dried cranberries, mixing well to combine.

5. Chill for a few hours before serving.

Makes 4 servings.

Nutrition per serving: 145 calories, 4.8 grams fat, 28 carbohydrates, 5 grams fiber, 8 grams protein

Did you know? ...

Kale is extremely rich in vitamin A, and is needed for maintaining healthy skin and vision. Kale is also one of the excellent vegetable sources for vitamin K, which helps bone growth and brain function. Extra virgin olive oil is a very healthy fat and is high in phenolic antioxidants, which helps prevent many diseases.

Crispy Corn Fritters

Ingredients:

½ cup all-purpose flour
2 Tbs. cornmeal
½ cup low-fat plain yogurt
2 large eggs
1 ½ cups fresh or frozen corn

1 tsp. baking powder
½ tsp. salt
1 Tbs. honey (optional)
½ tsp. smoked paprika (optional)
Non-stick cooking spray

Equipment:

Medium mixing bowl

Mixing spoon

Cutting board

Serrated knife

Non-stick skillet or frying pan

Whisk

Measuring cups

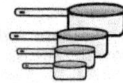

Measuring spoons

Spatula

Directions:

1. In a medium mixing bowl, whisk together the eggs and yogurt.

2. Add the cornmeal, flour, baking powder, salt, pepper, smoked paprika and honey (optional), mixing well.

3. Carefully stir in the corn. Your batter should be thick. Set aside or refrigerate until ready to make.

4. Prepare the skillet with non-stick cooking spray. Heat to medium.

5. Spoon about ¼ cup batter onto the hot pan. Cook for about 1 to 2 minutes or until golden brown on one side.

6. Flip the fritter over with a spatula. Cook for about 1 to 2 minutes more until done.

7. Repeat the steps until all corn fritters have been made.

8. Serve warm, with any of your favorite toppings, such as maple syrup, all fruit jam, yogurt or sour cream.

Makes 4 servings.

Nutrition per serving: 185 calories, 4 grams fat, 28 carbohydrates, 3 grams fiber, 9 grams protein

Did you know? ...

Fritters originated in the American South. Often served as side dishes or snacks, corn fritters are also called southern bread. The United States produces more than 40% of the world's corn, more than any other country.

Zucchini Parmesan Crisps

Ingredients:

4 medium zucchini,
  cut into ¼" round slices
2 Tbs. extra virgin olive oil
½ cup plain dry bread crumbs

½ cup freshly grated
  Parmesan cheese
1 tsp. salt
1 tsp. ground black pepper
Non-stick cooking spray

Equipment:

Small and
medium
mixing bowls

Grater

Mixing spoon

Measuring
cups

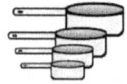

Cutting board

Measuring
spoons

Serrated knife

Spatula

Baking sheet

Oven
mitts

Directions:

1. Preheat oven to 425°F.

2. Grate the parmesan cheese if needed. Set aside.

3. Prepare the baking sheet by spraying it generously with non-stick cooking spray. Set aside.

4. Carefully cut the zucchini into ¼" round slices. In a medium mixing bowl, toss the zucchini with the olive oil. Set aside.

5. In the small mixing bowl, combine the Parmesan cheese, bread crumbs, salt and pepper.

6. Dip each round into the Parmesan mixture, coating evenly on both sides. Press the coating on so that it will stick to the zucchini.

7. Place each zucchini slice in a single layer onto the prepared baking sheet. Spray non-stick cooking spray over all the pieces.

8. Bake for a total of 20 to 25 minutes, until golden brown and crispy, turning over once after about 10 minutes.

9. Using oven mitts, carefully remove the baking sheet from the oven. Serve immediately.

Makes 4 servings.

Nutrition per serving: 105 calories, 5 grams fat, 8 carbohydrates, 2 grams fiber, 5 grams protein

Did you know? ...

One raw medium zucchini, including the skin, contains 56% of the daily-recommended amount of vitamin C.

Perfect Popovers

Ingredients:

1 Tbs. butter, melted
1 cup low fat milk
1 cup all-purpose flour

¼ tsp. salt
2 large eggs
Non-stick cooking spray

Equipment:

Medium mixing bowl

Measuring cups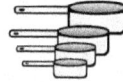

Mixing spoon

Measuring spoons

Grater

Muffin pan(s)

Whisk

Oven mitts

Directions:

1. Preheat oven to 425°F.

2. Spray the bottom and sides of the muffin pan(s) with cooking spray.

3. In a medium microwave safe mixing bowl, melt the butter in the microwave, about 20 seconds.

4. Carefully remove the bowl from the microwave and add the milk, flour and salt.

5. Add the eggs one at a time. Beat well with a whisk, until well combined.

6. Fill cups ¾ full. Bake for 10 minutes.

7. Reduce heat to 400°F. Bake for an additional 5 to 10 minutes, or until golden brown on top.

8. Using oven mitts, carefully remove muffin pan(s) from the oven.

9. Fill popovers with butter or any of your favorite preserves (optional).

Makes 12 popovers.

Nutrition per serving: 73.6 calories, 2 grams fat, 9.1 carbohydrates, 1 gram fiber, 3 grams protein

Did you know? ...

*Popovers originated in America in the mid 1800's.
The name "popover" comes from the fact that the batter swells
or "pops" over the top of the muffin pan while baking.*

Favorite BBQ Sauce

Ingredients:

1 cup ketchup
2 Tbs. brown sugar
¼ cup Worcestershire sauce
2 Tbs. apple cider vinegar

2 tsp. garlic powder
½ tsp. dried mustard
½ tsp. salt
1 dash hot pepper sauce (optional)

Equipment:

Medium
saucepan

Measuring
spoons

Mixing
spoon

Measuring
cups

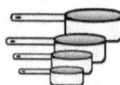

Directions:

1. In a medium saucepan over medium heat, stir together the ketchup, brown sugar, Worcestershire sauce, vinegar, garlic powder, dried mustard, salt and hot pepper sauce (optional).

2. Bring to a boil, stirring until ingredients are completely incorporated.

3. Reduce heat to low and gently simmer until flavors are combined and sauce has thickened, about 30 to 40 minutes.

4. Remove from heat and let the sauce cool to room temperature. If not using the sauce immediately, cover and refrigerate for up to 2 weeks.

5. Makes about 1¼ cups of sauce.

Nutrition per tablespoon: 32 calories, .5 grams fat, 7 grams carbohydrates, .1 gram protein

Did you know? ...

Barbecues have been a White House tradition since Thomas Jefferson was president. Lyndon B. Johnson, the 36th president of the United States, hosted the first barbecue at the White House that featured Texas-style barbecued ribs.

Salsa di Pomodoro
(*Italian Tomato Sauce*)

Ingredients:

¼ cup extra virgin olive oil
½ onion, minced
2 garlic cloves, minced
Crushed tomatoes, (28 oz.)
    fresh or canned

½ cup water
¼ cup fresh basil, chopped
2 tsp. dried oregano
1 tsp. salt
½ tsp. ground black pepper
2 tsp. sugar (optional)

Equipment:

Medium or large saucepan

Liquid measuring cup

Measuring spoons

Mixing spoon

Can opener

Serrated knife

Cutting board

Directions:

1. Open the tomatoes with a can opener, if needed. Set aside.

2. Peel and mince the onions and garlic. Carefully chop the fresh basil. Set aside.

3. In the saucepan, combine the olive oil and the onion. Cook over medium heat, until onions are soft.

4. Lower the heat to medium-low. Add the garlic and saute' for about a minute more, being careful not to burn the garlic.

5. Slowly add the crushed tomatoes, water, oregano, salt pepper and sugar (optional) to the saucepan. Continue to cook on medium-low heat for 20 to 30 minutes.

6. Add the chopped basil approximately 1 to 2 minutes prior to the sauce being complete. Taste for seasoning. Adjust if necessary.

   Makes 8 servings (about 4 cups).

Nutrition per serving: 68 calories, 1.9 grams fat, 8 grams carbohydrates, 1.4 grams protein

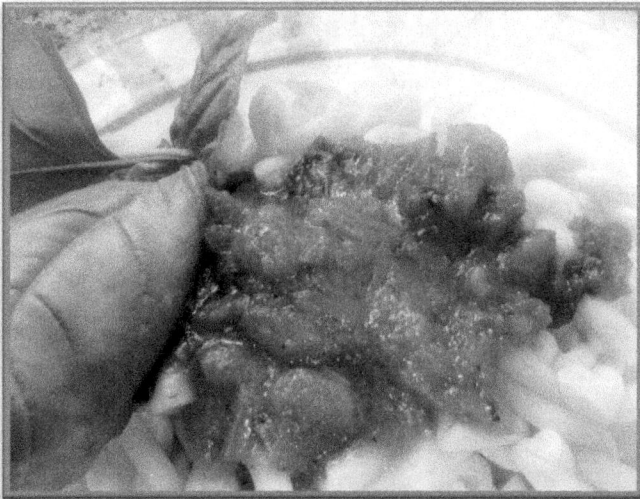

Did you know? ...

The tomato actually originated in Peru, and wasn't introduced to Italy until the sixteenth century. It finally became part of Italian cooking in the twentieth century.

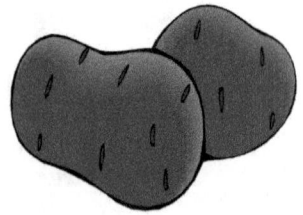

Meals in Minutes

Honey Grilled Shrimp - 70

Best Ever Beef Roast and Veggies - 72

Quick Salsa Verde Chicken Enchiladas - 74

Crispy Skin Salmon - 76

Spaghetti Carbonara - 78

Never-Fail Mac and Cheese - 80

Oven Herb Meatballs - 82

Monterey Ranch Chicken Bake - 84

Pulled Pork Sandwiches - 86

In-a-Pinch Favorite Lasagna - 88

Scan Me for a great cooking demo of a fast and healthy dinner idea!

Honey Grilled Shrimp

Ingredients:

1 bottle (8 oz.) Italian salad dressing*

1 cup honey

* or use our homemade recipe on page 100

2 lbs. uncooked large shrimp, peeled and deveined

1 cup bell peppers, chopped

1 large white onion, chopped

¼ cup fresh parsley, chopped

Non-stick cooking spray

Equipment:

Small mixing bowl

Liquid measuring cup

Cutting board

Measuring spoons

Serrated knife

Mixing spoon

Colander

Grill Pan

4 wooden skewers

Tongs

Baking pan

Large zip lock plastic bag

Directions:

1. Fill the baking pan half full with water. Soak the skewers for about a half hour. This will prevent the skewers from burning when grilling.

2. Cut the peppers and onion into 2 inch pieces. Carefully chop the parsley. Set aside.

3. Peel and devein the shrimp. Put the shrimp in a colander and rinse in cool water. Set aside.

4. In a small bowl, combine the salad dressing, honey and chopped parsley. Set aside ½ cup for basting.

5. Pour the remaining marinade into the zip lock bag. Add the shrimp, peppers and onions. Seal the bag and refrigerate for 30 minutes.

6. Drain and discard the marinade. Thread the shrimp and vegetables onto the skewers.

7. Prepare the grill pan by spraying it with non-stick cooking spray. Preheat the pan on medium heat.

8. Lay the skewers across the pan and grill for about 1 to 2 minutes on each side or until shrimp turns pink, basting frequently with the set aside marinade. Carefully use tongs to turn the skewers over.

Makes 4 servings.

Nutrition per serving: 65 calories, 5 grams fat, 4 carbohydrates, 2 grams fiber, 2 grams protein

scan here for a
cooking demo
of how to peel and
devein shrimp!

Did you know? ...

Shrimp is very high in protein and an excellent source of vitamin D and vitamin B12.

Best Ever Beef Roast and Veggies

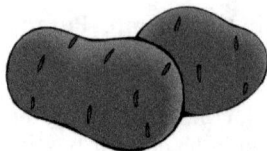

Ingredients:

2 lbs. boneless beef
   chuck roast
1 package (1.25 oz.) dry
   onion soup mix*

* or use our homemade
   recipe on page 92

½ cup water
4 large red potatoes
4 large carrots
1 large onion
1 Tbs. fresh rosemary (optional)
1 Tbs. fresh thyme (optional)

Equipment:

Cutting
board

Serrated
knife

9" x 13"
baking pan

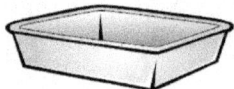

Mixing
spoon

Vegetable
scrubber

Vegetable
peeler

Liquid
measuring
cup

Aluminum
foil

Oven mitts

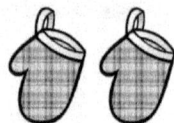

Directions:

1. Preheat the oven to 350°F.

2. Scrub and rinse the potatoes well. Carefully peel the carrots and onion. Cut the potatoes and onion into quarters. Cut the carrots in half. Chop the rosemary and thyme (optional). Set aside.

3. Prepare the baking pan by lining it with foil. Sprinkle about a tablespoon of the onion soup mix evenly onto the foil lined pan.

4. Place the beef roast in the pan. Add water and arrange the potatoes, onion and carrots around the meat.

5. Mix together the onion soup mix with the rosemary and thyme (optional). Sprinkle this mixture over the meat and vegetables.

6. Cover with additional foil. Bake for 2 hours or until beef and vegetables are roasted and tender.

7. Using oven mitts, carefully remove the pan from the oven. Serve hot with pan juices.

Makes 4 servings.

Nutrition per serving: 437 calories, 10 grams fat, 45 carbohydrates, 7 grams fiber, 38 grams protein

Did you know? ...

The Beef Roast or "Pot Roast" that most people associate today used to be called Yankee Pot Roast. That dish, made on the East Coast of the United States, evolved from the colonial era and was rump or round roast beef that was fresh and braised with vegetables, very similar to what we enjoy and eat today.

Quick Salsa Verde Chicken Enchiladas

Ingredients:

3 cups cooked rotisserie chicken, chopped

2 cups prepared salsa verde

8 Flour tortillas

3 cups low-fat Pepper Jack cheese or any favorite cheese, grated

Non-stick cooking spray

Equipment:

9" x 13" baking pan

Medium mixing bowl

Mixing spoon

Grater

Serrated knife

Cutting board

Oven mitts

Directions:

1. Preheat the oven to 350°F.

2. Chop the rotisserie chicken into bite size pieces. Set aside.

3. Grate the cheese if needed. Set aside.

4. Prepare the baking pan by spraying it with non-stick cooking spray. Spread ¼ cup of the salsa verde in the bottom of the pan. Set aside.

5. Combine the chopped chicken, 1 cup of the salsa verde and 2 cups of the grated cheese together in a medium mixing bowl.

6. Spoon about 1/3 cup mixture down the middle of each tortilla. Fold the tortillas over on each side and lay seam side down next to each other in the baking pan.

7. Top the enchiladas with remaining salsa verde and cheese.

8. Bake for 15 to 20 minutes, until heated through and cheese is melted.

9. Using oven mitts, carefully remove the pan from the oven.

Makes 8 large servings.

Nutrition per serving: 390 calories, 18 grams fat, 8.4 carbohydrates, 2 gram fiber, 34 grams protein

Did you know? ...

The history of enchiladas can be found in pre-Columbian times when the Mayas first invented the tortilla. In 1885, the word "Enchilada" first appeared in print, meaning "chili-filled".

Crispy Skin Salmon

Ingredients:

2 (6 oz. each) pieces wild salmon
  fillet with skin, 1" thick
3 Tbs. butter, softened
1 large lemon
1 tsp. Dijon mustard

1 Tbs. whole tarragon leaves
  or fresh dill
Kosher salt
Freshly cracked black pepper

Equipment:

Small
saucepan

Measuring
cups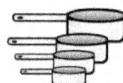

Mixing
spoon

Measuring
spoons

Serrated
knife

Grater

Cutting
board

Baking
sheet with
1" sides

Juicer

Oven mitts

Directions:

1. Using a grater, carefully zest 1 tablespoon of the lemon. Set aside.

2. Juice 2 Tbs. of the lemon. Chop the tarragon leaves or dill. Set aside.

3. Sprinkle the salmon with salt and pepper. Place skin side up and rub 1 ½ tablespoons of the softened butter all over the salmon skins.

4. Transfer the salmon, buttered side up, to the baking sheet. Chill in the refrigerator to firm the butter, about 20 minutes.

5. Preheat the broiler to high. Place the baking sheet about 6 inches from the heat source and cook until the skin is crispy and the fish is cooked through, about 7 to 8 minutes.

6. Using oven mitts, carefully remove the baking sheet from the oven.

7. In a small saucepan over moderate heat, whisk together the remaining 1 ½ tablespoons butter, lemon zest, lemon juice, mustard and tarragon or dill.

8. Serve the salmon with the sauce and a fresh lemon slice on the side for garnish, if desired.

Makes 2 servings.

Nutrition per serving: 359 calories, 22 grams fat, 4 carbohydrates, 0 grams fiber, 34 grams protein

Did you know? ...

Salmon is a highly nutritious food. Of course, it is high in protein, and the "good fats" but did you know that a 4 oz. serving of wild salmon provides a full day's requirement of vitamin D? It contains over half of the necessary B12, niacin, and selenium, and is an excellent source of B6 and magnesium.

Spaghetti Carbonara

Ingredients:

8 oz. uncooked spaghetti

½ lb. nitrate free bacon

4 large eggs, beaten

½ cup freshly grated parmesan cheese

½ cup milk

Salt and pepper to taste

Equipment:

Large pot or saucepan

Colander

Medium mixing bowl

Mixing spoon

Tongs

Non-stick skillet or frying pan

Measuring spoons

Liquid measuring cup

Grater

Directions:

1. Cook bacon until crispy. Drain and crumble into bite size pieces. Set aside.

2. Grate the parmesan cheese if needed. Set aside.

3. In a medium mixing bowl, combine the eggs, parmesan cheese. Set aside.

4. Cook spaghetti according to package directions. Drain the spaghetti and return to the cooking pot.

5. Carefully stir in the egg mixture. Quickly toss with the hot spaghetti and cook until egg mixture is done and coats the spaghetti, about a minute or two.

6. Stir in the crumbled bacon. Sprinkle with salt and pepper to taste.

7. Serve immediately with additional parmesan cheese, if desired.

Makes 4 servings.

Nutrition per serving: 584 calories, 32 grams fat, 44 carbohydrates, 1 grams fiber, 25 grams protein

Did you know? ...

In the mid 20th century, spaghetti carbonara was believed to be made as a hearty meal for the Italian charcoal workers. In parts of the United States it's called the "coal miner's spaghetti."

Never-Fail Mac and Cheese

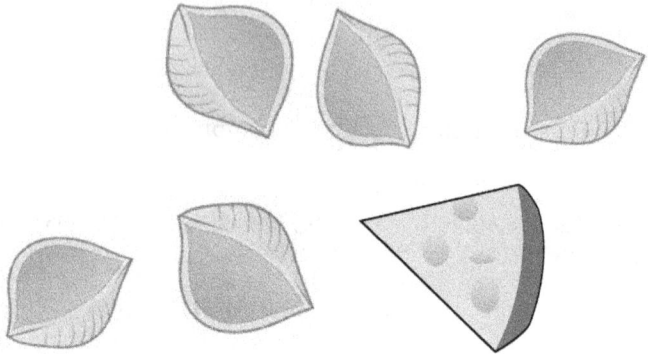

Ingredients:

2 ½ cups uncooked pasta shells
½ tsp. salt
½ tsp. ground black pepper
1 tsp. dry mustard (optional)

3 cups whole milk
2 cups sharp cheddar cheese
  at room temperature, grated

Equipment:

Large pot
or
saucepan

Mixing
spoon

Measuring
spoons

Liquid
measuring
cup

Grater

Directions:

1. Grate cheese, if needed. Set aside.

2. Combine uncooked pasta shells, milk, salt, pepper, and dry mustard (optional), in a large saucepan.

3. Cook over medium-high heat, stirring constantly until the pasta shells are tender, about 10 minutes.

4. Lower the heat, and gradually add the grated cheese, a half cup at a time.

5. Stir until cheese is melted and sauce is thickened.

6. Serve immediately.

Makes 6 (1 cup) servings.

Nutrition per serving: 385 calories, 18 grams fat, 25 carbohydrates, 1 gram fiber, 18 grams protein

Did you know? ...

Have you ever heard the song "Yankee Doodle" and wondered what the song meant by "stuck a feather in his hat, and called it "macaroni"? During the mid-18th century, a "macaroni" referred to a highly fashionable person. The song originated during the American Revolutionary War by the British. The joke was that the Americans (known as the Yankees) somehow believed that a feather in their hat was enough to make them fashionable.

Oven Herb Meatballs

Ingredients:

1 pound ground beef or chicken
½ small onion, minced
1 Tbs. fresh parsley, chopped
1 Tbs. fresh basil, chopped
1 Tbs. fresh rosemary, chopped
2 Tbs. tomato paste

½ cup plain dry bread crumbs
1 large egg, lightly beaten
½ tsp. kosher salt
¼ tsp. ground black pepper
¼ cup Parmesan cheese,
   freshly grated (optional)

Equipment:

Large mixing bowl

Mixing spoon

Cutting board

Serrated knife

Baking sheet with 1" sides

Grater

Measuring cups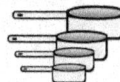

Measuring spoons

Parchment paper

Oven mitts

Directions:

1. Preheat oven to 375°.

2. Grate Parmesan cheese, if needed.

3. Mince the onion. Chop the rosemary, parsley and basil. Set aside.

4. Prepare a baking sheet by lining it with parchment paper. Set aside.

5. In a large mixing bowl, combine all the ingredients, one at a time, adding the ground beef or chicken last. Mix just enough to combine, but be careful not to over mix or you will have tough meatballs.

6. Using a spoon, portion out the meat mixture into 16 equal pieces and place on the prepared baking sheet.

7. After all the meatballs have been scooped onto the tray, wet your hands and carefully roll each piece into balls and arrange evenly on the tray.

8. Bake for 20-25 minutes, or until meatballs are golden brown on all sides.

9. Using oven mitts, carefully remove the baking sheet from the oven. Transfer to a sauce or serve immediately.

Makes 8 servings (2 meatballs per serving).

Nutrition per serving: 158 calories, 6 grams fat, 8 carbohydrates, 18 grams protein

Did you know? ...

The meatball is not only an Italian food. Many nations and cultures have their own, such as Greece, China, Sweden, Spain and India.

Monterey Ranch Chicken Bake

Ingredients:

1 lb. uncooked chicken breast tenders
½ cup milk
1 cup plain dry bread crumbs
1 cup Monterey Jack cheese, grated

2 Tbs. (1 oz. packet) ranch dressing mix*
Non-stick cooking spray

* or use our homemade recipe on page 98

Equipment:

Small and medium mixing bowls

Grater

Measuring spoons

Large baking sheet with 1" sides

Liquid measuring cup

Aluminum foil

Mixing spoon

Oven mitts

Directions:

1. Preheat oven to 350°F.

2. Prepare the baking sheet by lining it with foil and spraying with non-stick cooking spray. Set aside.

3. Grate cheese, if necessary. Set aside.

4. Combine the bread crumbs, cheese, and ranch dressing mix in a medium bowl. Pour the milk in a small bowl.

5. Dip the chicken pieces one at a time in the milk, then into the bread crumb mixture. Carefully arrange on the baking sheet and spray the top with non-stick cooking spray.

6. Bake the chicken for 40 to 45 minutes, turning over after 20 minutes.

7. Using oven mitts, carefully remove the baking sheet from the oven. The chicken is done when it's no longer pink in the center and the juices run clear. An instant read thermometer inserted into the center should read at least 165°F.

Makes 4 servings.

Nutrition per serving: 134 calories, 6.2 grams fat, 22 carbohydrates, 6 grams fiber, 8 grams protein

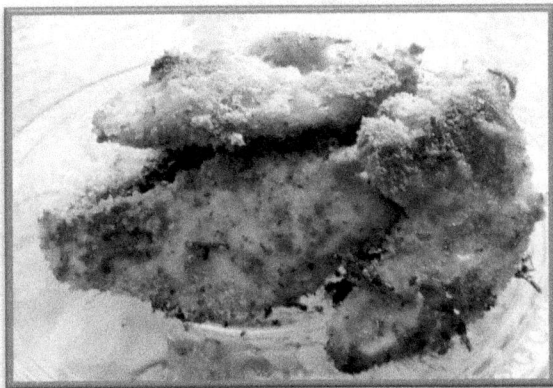

Did you know? ...

Chicken is a rich source of dietary protein, required to perform a number of vital functions in the body. Protein is also found to be essential for maintaining bone density and preventing osteoporosis. Chicken is widely used for consumption all over the world. Besides being rich in protein, it also contains many essential vitamins and minerals.

Pulled Pork Sandwiches

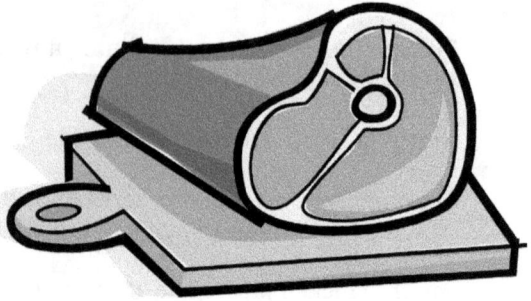

Ingredients:

3 lbs. pork shoulder roast
3 Tbs. smoked paprika
1 Tbs. dry mustard
3 Tbs. coarse salt
1 Tbs. garlic powder (optional)
1 Tbs. brown sugar (optional)

8 hamburger buns
2 cups bottled barbecue sauce*

*or use our homemade
recipe on page 64*

Equipment:

Small and
medium
mixing
bowl

9" x 13"
baking
pan

Measuring
spoons

Aluminum
foil

Liquid
measuring
cup

2 forks

Mixing
spoon

Oven
mitts

Directions:

1. Mix the paprika, dry mustard, salt, garlic power, and brown sugar together in a small bowl. Rub the spice blend all over the pork and marinate for as long as you have time for, as little as 1 hour or up to overnight, covered, in the refrigerator.

2. Preheat the oven to 300°F.

3. Put the pork in the baking pan and cover with foil. Bake for about 6 hours, or until it's falling apart and an instant-read thermometer inserted into the thickest part registers 170°F.

4. Using oven mitts, carefully remove the pork roast. Allow the meat to rest for about 10 minutes. Then, while still warm, take 2 forks and "pull" the meat to form shreds. Shred the pork by steadying the meat with 1 fork and pulling it away with the other.

5. Put the shredded pork in a medium size bowl. Pour about a cup of the barbeque sauce on the shredded pork and mix well to coat.

6. To serve, spoon the pulled pork mixture onto the bottom half of a hamburger bun. Serve with remaining sauce on the side.

7. Makes 8 servings.

Nutrition per serving: 280 calories, 9 grams fat, 29 carbohydrates, 2 grams fiber, 32 grams protein

Did you know? ...

Pork is the most widely eaten meat in the world, accounting for about 38% of meat production worldwide. Pork is popular throughout eastern Asia and the Pacific, where whole roast pig is a popular item in Pacific Island cuisine.

In-a-Pinch Favorite Lasagna

Ingredients:

1 lb. Italian sausage*
2 cups mozzarella cheese, grated
9 no-boil lasagna noodles

1 ½ cups ricotta cheese
1 (28 oz.) jar marinara sauce**

For a vegetarian version, replace the sausage with 1 cup frozen spinach, thawed and drained.

**or use our homemade recipe on page 66*

Equipment:

Non-stick skillet or frying pan

Grater

Measuring spoons

9" x 9" baking pan

Liquid measuring cup

Aluminum foil

Mixing spoon

Oven mitts

Directions:

1. Preheat oven to 350°F.

2. If using Italian sausage, cook in a skillet over medium heat, stirring to break up meat, until no longer pink, about 8 minutes. Drain well.

3. Mix cooked sausage or spinach, 1 ½ cups mozzarella cheese and ricotta cheese in medium bowl.

4. Place about ½ cup of the marinara sauce in the baking pan. Top with three lasagna noodles, then with one-third of cheese filling.

5. Repeat layers, ending with marinara sauce. Cover with foil and bake for 35 to 40 minutes, until hot and bubbly.

6. Sprinkle with remaining 1/2 cup mozzarella cheese and return to the oven.

7. Bake 5 to 10 minutes longer until cheese is melted.

Makes 6 servings.

Nutrition per serving: 217 calories, 8 grams fat, 25 carbohydrates, 5 grams fiber, 6 grams protein

Did you know? ...

Lasagna is believed to have originated in Italy. However, the term "lasagna" comes from the Greeks. The Italians used the word to refer to the dish in which lasagna is made. It wasn't long before the name of the food took on the name of the serving dish.

Make Your Own Healthy Mixes

Scan Me for quick and easy tips on how to sneak more veggies into your recipes!

Onion Soup and Dip Mix

Ingredients:

½ cup dried minced onions
8 beef bouillon cubes or
 8 tsp. beef bullion granules
2 tsp. onion powder

½ tsp. crushed celery seed
½ tsp. parsley flakes
½ tsp. paprika (optional)
½ tsp. black pepper (optional)

Equipment:

Medium
mixing
bowl

Measuring
cups

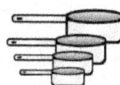

Mixing
spoon

Measuring
spoons

Directions:

1. In a medium mixing bowl, combine all the ingredients together. Mix together until well combined.

2. Store in an airtight container. 5 tablespoons equals a 1.25-ounce package of onion soup and dip mix.

    Makes 18 tablespoons.

Here are some great ways to use your mix:

-   Mix 5 tablespoons with 4 cups of water for soup.

-   Mix 2-3 tablespoons with 16 oz. of sour cream for dip.

-   Sprinkle on meat when cooking a beef roast.
    (See our recipe on page 72.)

-   Add a few tablespoons to a beef stew for added flavor.

Did you know? ...

The best thing to remove onion odor from your hands is to rub a stainless steel spoon all over them. It works great!

Ready Gravy Mix

Ingredients:

3 Tbs. beef or chicken
   bouillon granules

¾ cup plus 1 Tbs. all-purpose flour
2 tsp. ground black pepper

Equipment:

Small
mixing
bowl

Measuring
cups

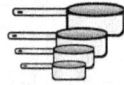

Mixing
spoon

Measuring
spoons

Directions:

1. In a small bowl, combine the bouillon, flour and black pepper.

2. Store in an airtight container until ready to use.

    Makes 32 servings (to make about 8 cups of gravy).

To Prepare Gravy:

2 Tbs. butter
2 Tbs. gravy mix
¾ cup cold water

- In a small saucepan, melt butter over low heat.

- Add 2 tablespoons gravy mix. Cook and stir until lightly browned, about 1 minute.

- Whisk in water until smooth. Bring to a boil; cook and stir for 2 minutes or until thickened.

Did you know? ...

This mix can be stored in an airtight container in a cool, dry place for up to 6 months. It's a quick and delicious gravy to accompany a meaty main dish or to pour over potatoes or noodles. We love it especially because it doesn't contain any artificial ingredients or preservatives, unlike most store-bought jars and packages.

Taco Seasoning

Ingredients:

6 Tbs. chili powder   2 Tbs. cumin
2 Tbs. garlic powder   3 Tbs. Kosher salt
2 Tbs. paprika

Equipment:

Small mixing bowl

Measuring cups

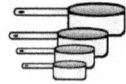

Mixing spoon

Measuring spoons

Directions:

1. In a small bowl, combine the chili powder, garlic powder, paprika, cumin and kosher salt together. Mix until well combined.

2. Store in an airtight container until ready to use.

   Makes about a half cup of taco seasoning.

Here are some great ways to use your seasoning:

- Add 2 tablespoons per pound of meat when making tacos.

- Add a few tablespoons to spice up refried beans.

- Sprinkle seasoning on baked potatoes for an extra zip.

- Add a few tablespoons to spaghetti sauce. Mix with your favorite pasta and grated cheddar cheese for amazing Mexican pasta!

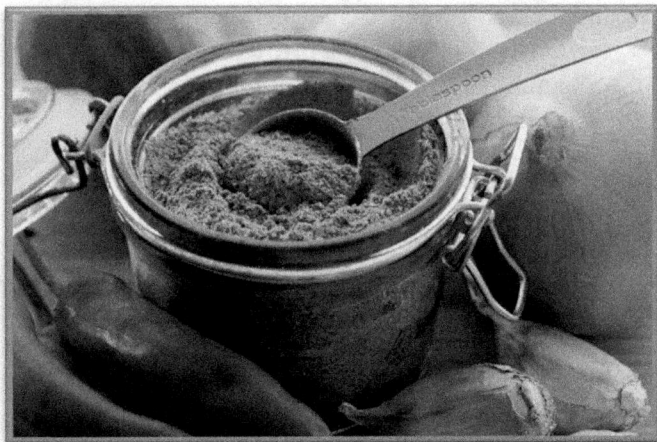

Did you know? ...

This mild taco seasoning has the flavor of traditional taco seasonings without all the heat. It's a great kid-friendly version of the old-time favorite. In addition, we love that it's all natural without any artificial flavors or preservatives.

Ranch Dip and Seasoning Mix

Ingredients:

1 cup dry buttermilk   1 tsp. garlic powder
2 Tbs. dried parsley   2 tsp. dried dill
2 Tbs. salt   2 tsp. dried onion flakes (optional)
2 tsp. onion powder   1 tsp. ground black pepper

Equipment:

Food
processor

Measuring
cups

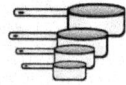

Mixing
spoon

Measuring
spoons

Directions:

1. In a small food processor, combine the dry buttermilk, parsley, dill, onion powder, garlic powder, dried onion flakes (optional), salt and pepper together.   Pulse about a minute, or until well combined.

2. Carefully pour the mix into an airtight container and store until ready to use.

   Makes about 1 ¼ cups, equivalent to about 18 envelopes of ranch dip and seasoning mix.

Here are some great ways to use your Ranch mix:

- Mix 2 to 3 tablespoons with 16 oz. of sour cream to make a delicious ranch dip.

- Add 1 to 2 tablespoons with 1 cup mayonnaise and 1 cup buttermilk to make a creamy ranch salad dressing.

- Mix a few tablespoons with bread crumbs for a great chicken breading before baking. (See our recipe on page 84.)

- Sprinkle on hot popped popcorn for a tasty treat!

Did you know? ...

This mix can be stored for up to 12 months and added to other ingredients to make homemade ranch dip or dressing. It has no artificial ingredients and no MSG unlike many other ready-made seasoning mixes. Best of all, it tastes amazing!

Italian Dressing and Seasoning Mix

Ingredients:

4 Tbs. oregano
2 Tbs. garlic powder
2 Tbs. onion powder
2 Tbs. dried parsley flakes
2 tsp. dried basil

1 Tbs. ground black pepper
2 Tbs. salt
1 tsp. celery seed (optional)
½ tsp. teaspoon thyme (optional)
½ tsp. sugar (optional)

Equipment:

Small
mixing
bowl

Measuring
cups

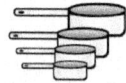

Mixing
spoon

Measuring
spoons

Directions:

1. In a small bowl, combine all of the ingredients together. Mix until well combined.

2. Store in an airtight container until ready to use.

   Makes about ¾ cup of seasoning mix.

Here are some great ways to use your mix:

- Mix 2 tablespoons with ¼ cup vinegar and ½ cup extra virgin olive oil to make a zesty Italian dressing.

- Mix a few tablespoons in spaghetti sauce for added flavor.

- Add to pasta salad or sprinkle on fresh sliced tomatoes.

Did you know? ...

This convenient mix is for all recipes that call for Italian dressing or seasoning. It is has all natural ingredients with no preservatives, and stays fresh for about 12 weeks in an airtight container.

Condensed Cream Soup

Ingredients:

3 Tbs. butter
2-3 cloves garlic, minced
3 Tbs. white or whole wheat flour
½ tsp. salt

¼ tsp. ground black pepper
½ tsp. celery seed (optional)
1 ¾ cups chicken broth
¾ cup milk

Equipment:

Medium
saucepan

Measuring
cups

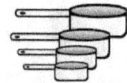

Mixing
spoon

Can opener

Measuring
spoons

Cutting
board

Serrated
knife

Directions:

1. Carefully peel and mince the garlic. Open the chicken broth with a can opener if needed. Set aside.

2. In the saucepan over medium heat, cook garlic in butter until soft.

3. Stir in flour, celery seed (optional), salt and pepper. Slowly stir in chicken broth and milk.

4. Simmer over medium-low heat until thickened.

5. Makes about 2 cups, equivalent to a regular can of condensed soup.

Here are some great variations:

- Cream of Mushroom soup - Add a handful of minced mushrooms.

- Cream of Broccoli soup - Add a handful of minced broccoli.

- Cream of Celery soup - Add a handful of minced celery.

Did you know? ...

This is a great multi-purpose recipe to replace condensed canned soup in any recipe that calls for it. It's super easy and a lot healthier than store bought canned soups.

Healthy Oatmeal Packets

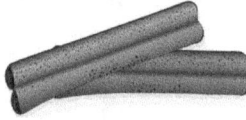

Ingredients:

42 oz. container whole
grain quick oats
1 lb. brown sugar
¼ cup ground cinnamon

1 cup ground flax seeds
1 cup raisins or dried cranberries or
any favorite dried fruit (optional)
1 cup chocolate chips or nuts
(optional)

Equipment:

Small
mixing
bowl

Measuring
cups

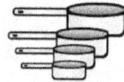

Measuring
spoons

Mixing
spoon

30 small
zip lock
baggies

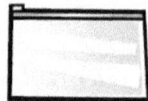

Directions:

1. Measure and pour ½ cup of the quick oats, 1 to 2 tablespoons of brown sugar, and ½ tsp. ground cinnamon into each of the 30 baggies.

2. Add a few tablespoons of the ground flax seeds, raisins, dried fruit or chocolate chips (optional) to each baggie also.

3. Seal all of the baggies. These can be stored for up to 6 months.

   Makes 30 oatmeal packets.

Here are some great ways to use your Packets:

- Add 1 cup of hot water or milk to one packet to make a quick and easy, healthy bowl of oatmeal.

- Mix 1 packet with a ½ mashed banana and 1 large egg for a healthy oatmeal pancake batter.

- Mix 1 packet with a tablespoon of butter. Sprinkle over a cored apple, cut in half. Bake at 350°F oven for 30 minutes, or until apple is tender and topping is golden.

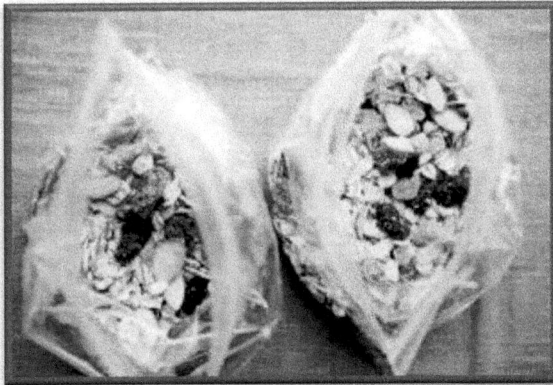

Did you know? ...

Oatmeal is a very healthy whole grain to get your motor running for the day. Flax seeds are a great source of fiber and contains concentrated amounts of alpha-linolenic acid (ALA), an omega-3 fat. These packets are very easy to make, significantly cheaper and far tastier than the store bought ones.

Ready-Made Pancake and Baking Mix

Ingredients:

4 cups whole wheat flour
6 cups all-purpose flour
2 ½ cups powdered milk

½ cup granulated sugar
4 Tbs. baking powder
2 Tbs. salt

Equipment:

Large mixing bowl

Measuring cups

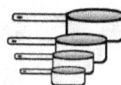

Mixing spoon

Measuring spoons

Directions:

1. In a large mixing bowl, gently mix all of the ingredients together.

2. Pour the mixture in an airtight container. This pancake mix can be stored for up to three months.

   Makes 8 batches (about 6 to 8 pancakes per batch).

Here are some great ways to use your mix:

1. Combine 1 ½ cups mix with 1 cup water, 1 large egg, and 2 Tbs. oil to make a quick and easy pancake batter. Pour ¼ cup of batter onto a greased hot griddle. Turn when bubbles form on top of pancakes.

2. To make waffles, combine 1½ cups mix with 2 large eggs and 2 Tbs. oil. Bake in a preheated waffle iron according to manufacturer's directions.

3. Mix 2 ½ cups mix with 1 large egg, ½ cup sugar, ¾ cup water, ¼ cup canola oil, and 1½ cups fresh or frozen blueberries to make blueberry muffins. Pour ¾ full in greased muffin pans. Bake for 20 minutes at 350°F, or until golden brown on top.

Did you know? ...

This mix will sure to become one of your all time family favorites. These pancakes always come out fluffy and full of flavor. They also can be made in advance and frozen, then put in the toaster for a quick breakfast on the go!

Chocolate Pudding Mix

Ingredients:

½ granulated sugar
½ cup instant Clear Jel

½ cup unsweetened cocoa powder
½ tsp. salt

Equipment:

Blender

Mixing
spoon

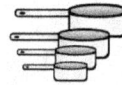

Measuring
cups

Measuring
spoons

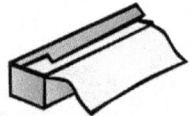

Plastic wrap

Directions:

1. Combine sugar, clear jel, cocoa powder and salt in a blender. Run on high about 30 seconds to combine and grind the sugar to powder.

2. When ready to make pudding, add 2 cups cold milk to the mix using an electric mixer or blender, mix until well combined, about a minute.

3. Portion pudding into ½ cup servings. Place a piece of plastic wrap on the surface of each portion and refrigerate for 30 minutes.

   Makes 4 (1/2 cup) servings.

Here are some other great ways to use your mix:

- Pour prepared pudding into paper cups. Insert a popsicle stick and freeze until firm to make quick and easy pudding pops.

- Combine pudding mix with ¾ cup butter and 1¼ cups all-purpose flour to make a delicious egg-free cookie dough. Drop by rounded teaspoonfuls onto baking sheet and bake at 350°F for 10-12 minutes.

- Add pudding mix to your favorite chocolate cake mix before baking, for an extra rich and moist cake.

Did you know? ...

Instant Clear Jel is a modified cornstarch that is used in "cold" products like pudding and pie glazes. It is not usually sold in stores, but can easily be found online. The non-GMO "Instant" jel is best for this recipe.

Favorite Cake Mix

Ingredients:

8 cups all-purpose flour
4 cups granulated sugar
4 Tbs. baking powder

2 cups non-fat dry milk
2 cups unsweetened cocoa
powder (optional)*

to make chocolate cake mix

Equipment:

Large
mixing
bowl

Measuring
cups

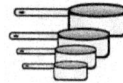

Mixing
spoon

Measuring
spoons

4 large
zip lock
baggies

Directions:

1. Combine flour, sugar, baking powder, and non-fat dry milk, and cocoa powder (optional).

2. Divide the mixture equally, about 3½ to 4 cups into each of the 4 zip lock baggies.

3. These cake mixes can be stored for up to 6 month in the refrigerator, freezer or pantry.

   Makes 4 cake mix recipes.
   (equivalent to 4 standard, 18.25 oz. store bought yellow cake mixes)

Making the Cake:

1. Place cake mix recipe in a large mixing bowl. Add ¾ cup water, ½ cup softened butter, 3 large eggs and 1 tsp. vanilla extract.

2. Using an electric mixer, beat until combined, about 2 to 3 minutes.

3. Pour into desired pan(s) and bake per instructions below.

Bake at 350°F, using these baking times:

- 2 (8" or 9") round cake pans, greased --- 20 to 25 minutes

- 9" x 13" baking pan, greased --- 35 to 40 minutes

- 24 cupcakes with paper liners --- 12 to15 minutes

- Standard bundt pan, greased --- 45 to 50 minutes

Cake is done when a toothpick inserted in the center comes out clean.

Did you know? ...

Instead of using dry milk in this mix, you can always leave it out and replace the water in the recipe with milk instead. This is a great homemade recipe to replace commercial cake mixes, and it doesn't have all the additives, preservatives and artificial colorings that store bought varieties have.

Clean Eating Desserts

Scan Me for a cooking demo of how to make a quick and healthy kid-pleasing dessert!

Inside-Out
Chocolate Strawberries

Ingredients:

20 to 24 fresh strawberries	1 cup chocolate chips, semi-sweet, dark, or white

Equipment:

Small microwave safe glass bowl

Measuring cups

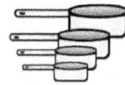

Mixing spoon

Measuring spoons

Zip lock baggie

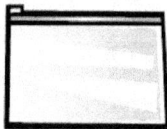

Serrated knife

Small cutting board used for fruits and vegetables

Directions:

1. Carefully rinse the strawberries and wipe well with a paper towel.

2. Cut off the top of each strawberry, and use a small ¼ teaspoon to scoop out the white part inside the strawberry.

3. Use a paper towel to carefully dry the inside of the strawberries. This will help the chocolate stick better to the strawberries.

4. Melt the chocolate in a small microwave safe glass bowl. Start with 30 seconds, stir and return to the microwave for 30-second intervals until the chocolate is melted.

5. Carefully pour or spoon the chocolate into a zip lock baggie. Squeeze out all the air and zip shut. Use a pair of scissors to cut off ¼" corner of the bag.

6. Pipe the chocolate into the holes of the strawberries. Let the chocolate set for a few minutes before eating. These also can be refrigerated for a few hours before serving.

Makes 20 to 24 servings.

Nutrition per serving: 56 calories, 2.3 grams fat, 6 carbohydrates, 2 grams fiber, 1 gram protein

Did you know? ...

Eight strawberries have more vitamin C than an orange. That's 140% of our daily-recommended amount.

Peanut Butter Chocolate Chip Cookies

Ingredients:

1 cup all natural peanut butter
½ cup granulated sugar
1 large egg

2 tsp. baking soda
1 cup chocolate chips
Non-stick cooking spray

Equipment:

Large mixing bowl

Baking sheet

Mixing spoon

Spatula

Measuring cups

Oven mitts

Measuring spoons

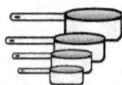

Directions:

1. Preheat oven to 350°F.

2. Prepare the baking sheet by spraying it with non-stick cooking spray.

3. In a medium mixing bowl, mix together the peanut butter, sugar, egg and baking soda until well combined.

4. Add the chocolate chips, mixing well until a soft dough forms.

5. Drop cookie dough a tablespoon at a time on the baking sheet and flatten just a little bit.

6. Bake for 9 to 10 minutes, or until cookies are crisp around the edges and golden on top.

7. Using oven mitts, carefully remove the baking sheet from the oven.

8. Let the cookies set for about 5 minutes before removing with a spatula.

Makes 16 cookies.

Nutrition per cookie: 92 calories, 4.2 grams fat, 9 carbohydrates, 1 gram fiber, 3 grams protein

Did you know? ...

Peanut butter is rich in vitamin B3 (Niacin), which is good for the nervous system and helps in the formation of healthy skin, hair and nails.

Fruity Dessert Crepes

Ingredients:

1 cup all-purpose flour   ¼ tsp. salt
½ cup milk   2 Tbs. butter, melted
½ cup water   ½ cup all-fruit jam
2 large eggs   Non-stick cooking spray

Equipment:

Medium mixing bowl

Whisk

Mixing spoon

6" non-stick skillet

Measuring cups

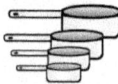

Measuring spoons

Spatula

Directions:

1. Combine flour, milk, water, eggs, salt and butter.

2. Prepare the skillet by spraying it with non-stick cooking spray. Heat the skillet to medium heat.

3. Pour about ¼ cup of batter in the skillet. Tilt the pan in a circular motion so that the batter coats the surface evenly.

4. Cook the crepe for about 2 minutes, until the bottom is very light brown. Loosen with a spatula. Turn the crepe over and briefly cook the other side, about 20 seconds more.

5. To remove the crepe from the pan, carefully invert the skillet over a plate and the crepe should easily fall away from the pan.

6. Repeat steps 2 through 5 with the remaining batter.

7. Fill crepes with your favorite all fruit jam and top with fresh whipped cream if desired.

Makes 8 crepes.

Nutrition per crepe: 83 calories, 2.8 grams fat, 8 carbohydrates, 3.2 grams protein

scan here for a
cooking demo
of how to make
a crepe!

Did you know? ...

A crepe is a French pancake. They are often spread with jam, fruit, whipped cream or rolled in a sweet sauce and served as a dessert. Crepes also may be filled with meat, chicken or cheese and served as an entrée.

Apple Pie Dip and Chips

Ingredients:

4 cups diced apples, peeled and cored
1 large lemon
3 Tbs. brown sugar

2 tsp. ground cinnamon
2 tsp. cornstarch, dissolved in 2 tsp. water
All natural tortilla chips

Equipment:

Medium saucepan

Measuring spoons

Small mixing bowl

Juicer

Mixing spoon

Serrated knife

Measuring cups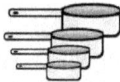

Small cutting board

Directions:

1. Cut the lemon in half and juice to make 2 Tbs. lemon juice. Set aside.

2. Mix the cornstarch with 2 teaspoons of water in a small bowl. Set aside.

3. Carefully peel and core the apples. Dice into bite size pieces.

4. In a medium saucepan, combine the apples, lemon juice, brown sugar and cinnamon.

5. Cook on medium heat for a few minutes until apples begin to soften.

6. Add the cornstarch mixture and continue to cook until it starts to boil and sauce has thickened, about 2 minutes.

7. Serve the apple pie dip warm or cold with all natural tortilla chips.

Makes 4 servings (½ cup per serving).

Nutrition per serving: 54 calories, 1 gram fat, 16 carbohydrates, 2 grams fiber

scan here for a cooking demo of how to peel, core and dice an apple!

Did you know? ...

*Apples are a great source of the fiber pectin.
One apple has 5 grams of fiber.*

Extreme Bread Pudding

Ingredients:

1 loaf challah or egg bread   3 cups heavy cream
3 large eggs   ½ cup semi sweet chocolate chips
½ cup granulated sugar   Non-stick cooking spray

Equipment:

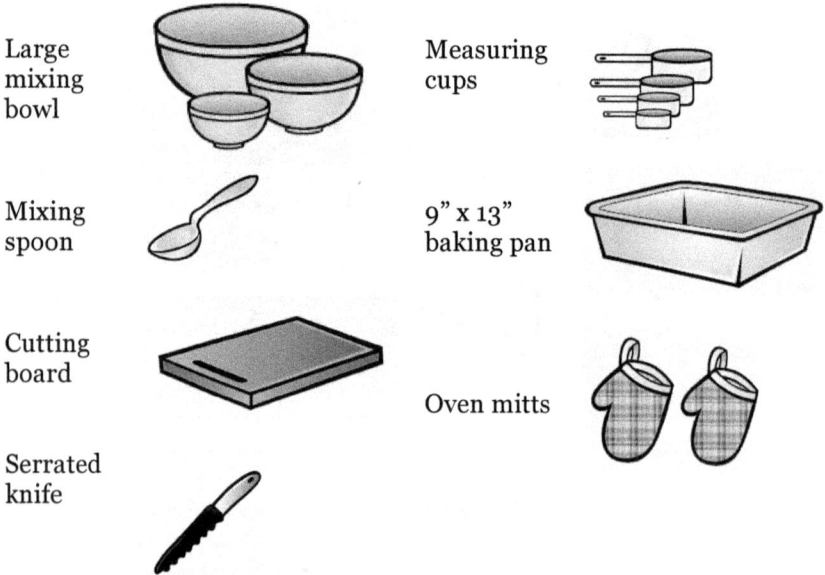

Large mixing bowl

Mixing spoon

Cutting board

Serrated knife

Measuring cups

9" x 13" baking pan

Oven mitts

Directions:

1. Preheat oven to 350°F.

2. Prepare the baking pan by spraying the bottom and sides with non-stick cooking spray. Set aside.

3. Cut the loaf of bread into rough 1-inch chunks. Set aside.

4. Whisk the eggs, sugar, and cream together in a large mixing bowl until the sugar has fully dissolved.

5. Line the baking pan with half the bread cubes, then sprinkle evenly with half of the chocolate chips. Repeat with the remaining bread cubes and chocolate chips.

6. Pour the egg mixture over the bread and let the pudding rest for 10 minutes to allow the bread to absorb the liquid.

7. Bake for about 30 minutes, until the pudding is bubbling around the edges and just starting to brown on top.

8. Using oven mitts, carefully remove the pan from the oven. Serve warm with fresh whipped cream if desired.

    Makes 12 servings.

Nutrition per serving: 187 calories, 6.2 grams fat, 28.6 carbohydrates, 3 grams fiber, 7.3 grams protein

Did you know? ...

Food historians generally attribute the origin of basic bread pudding to frugal cooks who did not want to waste stale bread. Since very early times it was common practice to use stale, hard bread or even crumbs when making bread pudding.

Raspberry-Pineapple Chia Popsicles

Ingredients:

2 cups frozen raspberries
2 cups frozen pineapple, chopped

1 cup chia seeds
1 cup orange juice
½ cup water

Equipment:

Blender

12 popsicle
sticks

Mixing
spoon

12 paper cups

Measuring
spoons

Liquid
measuring cup

Directions:

1. Combine raspberries, pineapple, chia seeds, orange juice and water in the blender.

2. Cover with a lid and blend on low speed until smooth, about a minute.

3. Carefully pour about ½ cup of mixture into the paper cups.

4. Insert the popsicle sticks into each cup and freeze until firm.

5. Peel off the paper cup before eating.

   Makes 12 servings.

Nutrition per serving: 112 calories, 3 grams fat, 12 carbohydrates, 11 grams fiber, 3 grams protein

scan here to learn more about the health benefits of Chia seeds!

Did you know? ...

Berries are a rich source of antioxidants. Chia seeds are an amazing super food! They have more Omega-3 fatty acids than any other plant food.

3 Ingredient Energy Bars

Ingredients:

1 cup toasted seed or nuts   1 cup pitted dates (12-15 whole)
1 cup dried fruit

Equipment:

Food processor

Measuring cups

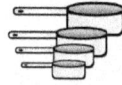

Mixing spoon

Measuring spoons

Serrated knife

Plastic wrap or wax paper

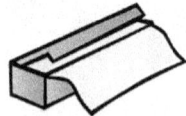

Cutting board

Directions:

1. Combine the seeds or nuts, dried fruit, and dates in a food processor. Pulse a few times and process for about a minute. Scrape the edges of the bowl and beneath the blade to make sure nothing is sticking.

2. Process continuously until a ball is formed, about 2 to 3 minutes.

3. Wrap the dough in plastic wrap or wax paper and refrigerate until chilled, about an hour.

4. When the dough is chilled, press with your hands until it forms a thick square, roughly 8" x 8" in size. Wrap and chill again for at least another hour or overnight.

5. Unwrap the chilled dough and transfer to a cutting board. Cut into 6 large bars or 12 small squares, as desired. Wrap each bar in plastic wrap or wax paper.

6. Store in the refrigerator for several weeks or in the freezer for up to three months.

    Makes 6 large bars.

    Try these variations: add ½ cup of unsweetened shredded coconut, chia seeds, chocolate chips, cacao nibs, cocoa powder, protein powder, ground cinnamon, ground nutmeg or lemon zest.

Approximate nutrition per serving: 86 calories, 12 grams fat, 36 carbohydrates, 6 gram fiber, 7 grams protein

Did you know? ...

Dates are high in vitamin A with antioxidants that keep eyes healthy. Dates also contain potassium, which is high in electrolytes that regulate blood pressure and heart rate.

Dairy-Free Pumpkin Ice Cream

Ingredients:

30 oz. full fat coconut milk, cold
1 cup pumpkin puree, cold
½ cup pure maple syrup

2 tsp. pumpkin pie spice
1 tsp. vanilla extract

Equipment:

Blender

Medium mixing bowl

Mixing spoon

Liquid measuring cup

Measuring spoons

Directions:

1. Combine the coconut milk, pumpkin, maple syrup, pumpkin pie spice and vanilla in the blender.

2. Secure the lid and blend until smooth, about 1 to 2 minutes.

3. Pour the mixture into a medium mixing bowl and put in the freezer for 30 minutes.

4. Remove the bowl from the freezer and stir the ice cream. Continue this step every half hour for the next 3 hours.

5. Cover the ice cream and keep in the freezer until ready to serve.

Makes 8 (½ cup) servings.

Nutrition per serving: 312 calories, 16 grams fat, 14 carbohydrates, 7 grams fiber, 8 grams protein

Did you know? ...

Pumpkin is one of the most nutritious fruits. 1 cup of pumpkin offers 145% of your daily requirements of vitamin A.

Best Ever Brownie Cake

Ingredients:

4 large eggs
8 oz. pitted dates (about 25)
½ cup water
1 tsp. salt

1 cup unsweetened cocoa powder
½ cup coconut oil or butter, melted
Non-stick cooking spray

Equipment:

Small and medium mixing bowls

Medium saucepan

Whisk

Food processor

Mixing spoon

Colander

Measuring cups

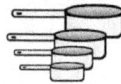

8" x 8" baking pan

Measuring spoons

Oven mitts

Directions:

1. Melt the coconut oil or butter in a small microwave safe bowl, about 30 seconds. Set aside.

2. In a medium saucepan, cover the dates with ½ cup water. Heat on medium-high heat until the water begins to boil.

3. Turn off the heat and allow the dates to soak for at least 30 minutes, or until really soft.

4. Strain the water and blend the dates in a food processor, adding the reserved liquid until you have about 1 ½ cups. Set aside to cool.

5. Preheat the oven to 350°F.

6. Prepare the baking pan by spraying the bottom and sides with non-stick cooking spray.

7. In the medium mixing bowl, whisk the eggs, date puree, cocoa powder, melted coconut oil or butter, and salt together.

8. Pour the mixture into the prepared baking pan.

9. Bake for about 30 minutes or until a toothpick comes out clean in the middle and center springs back to the touch.

Makes 9 servings.

Nutrition per serving: 227 calories, 12.2 grams fat, 15 carbohydrates, 1 gram fiber, 5.2 gram protein

Did you know? ...

Small amounts of cocoa can reduce cholesterol in the blood and can lower blood pressure. Cocoa is also very rich in agents that can enhance the production of various feel-good chemicals in your brain.

Best Ever
Chocolate Frosting

Ingredients:

2 cans coconut milk,
full-fat, chilled

6 oz. dark chocolate, chopped
2 tsp. honey

Equipment:

Small and
medium
mixing bowls

Measuring
cups

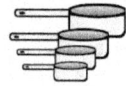

Mixing
spoon

Measuring
spoons

Can opener

Electric
mixer

Directions:

1. Melt the chocolate in a small microwave safe mixing bowl, stirring every 20 to 30 seconds until just melted.

2. Open cans of coconut milk and separate the hard cream from the top into a medium mixing bowl.

3. Measure about 1 ½ cups into the bowl and beat on medium-high for about 2 minutes, or until the lumps have been removed and it is light and fluffy.

4. Slowly add the melted chocolate and honey, mixing well.

5. Allow the frosting to chill in the refrigerator until firm enough to frost the cake.

    Makes 2 cups (¼ cup per serving).

Nutrition per serving: 97 calories, 8.3 grams fat, 5 carbohydrates, 1 gram fiber, 1.4 grams protein

Did you know? ...

Coconut milk is highly nutritious and contains healthy fats that protect us from bacterial and viral infections.

Recipe Index

About the Author

Kelly Lambrakis is an editor, writer and a health food enthusiast. She is a widow and has three young boys, living in Southern California. She has always loved spending time in the kitchen. Her mother taught her how to cook at a very young age. As a little girl, they loved making favorite recipes together, including homemade treats for family and friends to enjoy. Years later, she continued that tradition, making it a priority to include her children in the kitchen, like her mother did, in hopes that her boys would enjoy cooking too.

Kelly is the author of the popular Cooking with Kids, Boys Can Cook Too! and the Cookin' Up Fun! series of cookbooks. With her passion for healthy eating, she believes that it's not difficult or time consuming to eat clean, healthy foods, and to teach our children to do the same. Her series of Cooking with Kids interactive cookbooks are sold in Paperback and in Kindle format in hopes that many adults and children will easily access quick and healthy recipes that anyone can make. Her most recent cookbooks range from healthy quick snacks, allergy sensitive recipes, including easy soups, lunchbox favorites, and 5 ingredient healthy meals that the whole family can enjoy, even during busy, active schedules.

Here are some other Cooking with Kids books you may like!

Cooking with Kids - Healthy Snacks
*Quick and Healthy Recipes to make
with Kids in 10 minutes or less!*

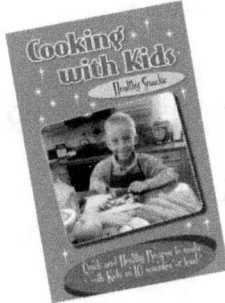

Cooking with Kids - Allergy Free
*Favorite Whole Food Recipes for
Allergy Friendly and Low Sugar Cooking*

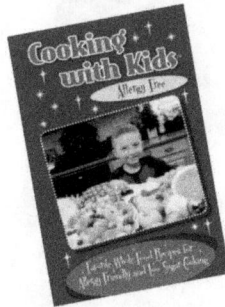

Cooking with Kids - Cookies and More!
*Sweet Treats and Healthy Options
for Kids that love to Bake*

Fundraising Opportunities

We Love to Help!

Are you interested in raising money to help
a worthy cause in your community?

We support schools, youth groups and clubs,
as well as charitable non-profits.

Visit

www.CookingWithKids4YourHealth.com

to learn more!

www.ingramcontent.com/pod-product-compliance
Lightning Source LLC
LaVergne TN
LVHW021507080426
835509LV00018B/2428